D0604803

Café Spice Namaste

Café Spice Namaste

Modern Indian Cooking

Cyrus Todiwala

SOMA
san francisco

Acknowledgments

I would like firstly to thank my wife Pervin for her unfaltering support and her faith in all that I do. Also for being so patient while I worked on this book and trying to sleep under the glare of the computer screen while I punched away at the keys until the wee hours of the morning.

A big thank you goes to my parents, who have given me all the help that I ever needed, from spending hours by my bedside when I was an asthmatic child, to enduring sleepless nights during my early baking days and supporting me in my choice of career despite their disappointment in it. I hope that I have done them proud; they are the greatest parents one could wish for.

Thanks also to Tony Hewitt, our good and dear friend, who tried out all the recipes in this book and helped me adjust them where necessary to make them suitable for use in the home. Not forgetting my team of chefs, who had to take on an additional burden while I wrote this book, particularly my wonderful head chefs Angelo and Mathias.

Lastly thanks to all the members of our team, old and new, at Café Spice Namaste, and to my business partners Michael and Martin, who have helped me to make Café Spice all that it is today.

Thank you all.

NOTE ON THE RECIPES
Unless otherwise stated, all recipes serve 4, and oil is sunflower oil.

Text © 1998 Cyrus Todiwala
North American Text © 1998 Soma Books
Photographs © 1998 Ebury Press

All rights reserved. No part of this book may be used or reproduced in any manner whatsoever without the written permission of the Publisher, except in the case of brief quotations in critical articles and reviews.

The right of Cyrus Todiwala to be identified as the author of this work has been asserted by him in accordance with the Copyright, Designs and Patents Act 1988

First published 1998 in Great Britain by Ebury Press. North American edition published 1998 by SOMA Books, by arrangement with Ebury Press.

SOMA Books is an imprint of Bay Books & Tapes, Inc., 555 De Haro St., No. 220, San Francisco, CA 94107.

Library of Congress Cataloging-In-Publication Data on file with the publisher

ISBN 1-57959-028-4

Printed in Singapore
10 9 8 7 6 5 4 3 2 1

Distributed to the trade by Publishers Group West

For the Ebury Press edition:
Editor: Jane Middleton
Photography: Philip Webb
Stylist: Roísín Nield
Home Economist: Sunil Vijayakar
Illustrations: Rosemary Woods

For the SOMA edition:
Publisher: James Connolly
Art Director: Jeffrey O'Rourke
Editorial Director: Clancy Drake
Jacket Design: Randall Lockridge
Production: Patrick David Barber
North American Editor: Jane Horn
Proofreader: Rita Siglain

Contents

Introduction

I often think of my first adventures in cooking, when I was just eight or nine years old and living in Bombay. I used to steal Mum's *chapatis*, caramelize them in sugar or butter until crisp and then sell them for five *paisa* each to my cousins and sister. Mum's *chapatis*, her butter, her sugar, her gas stove—and my profits.

When I was twelve I attempted to make my first custard by adding custard powder to boiling milk. I wanted to give my mother a surprise when she came home, but even she couldn't remedy the disastrous mess that ensued. Some of my greatest learning experiences and inspirations came from watching my mother—from the basics of chopping an onion to making a few of the recipes in this book.

My father used to talk to me about food and drink in the days of the Maharajas, and about the medicinal properties of various ingredients. He himself cooked only a few dishes, but they were always extremely good. He wanted me to go into mechanical engineering, which was his specialty. Being a chef is considered a lowly profession in India, and when I chose it as a career my parents had to face a certain amount of mockery from friends to whom chefs were merely domestic hands.

It was while I was at boarding school that I regularly visited an uncle's hotel, and this is when I decided to work in catering. After completing a diploma in hotel management I took a job at the Taj Mahal Hotel in Bombay as an apprentice cook. At that time kitchen apprentices were expected to endure the most appalling hardships, including both physical and verbal abuse, and all for a salary that I would be ashamed to offer even the greenest of recruits. But at least the job gave me the opportunity to acquire the knowledge and skills I needed.

At the same time I also ran my own little bakery from home, often baking until 4 AM before getting up at 7 to leave for a day's work. I spent almost fifteen years with the Taj group, eventually becoming executive chef of its prestigious hotel complex in Goa. My training took place in the Continental kitchens (there was a separate kitchen for Indian food), where I specialized in French cuisine, especially *patisserie* and baking. However, after I moved to Goa I began to take more interest in Indian cooking and to research it thoroughly. I became convinced that what my country had to offer was far greater than the rest of the world's cuisines put together, and that I could never master it in ten lifetimes.

Indian cuisine is very diverse, with immense regional, cultural and religious variations, and it can be as simple or as intricate as you like. Dating back long before the earliest European cuisines were established, over the centuries it has acquired a scientific and medical dimension. Because of India's inhospitable climate, ways of preserving food with herbs and spices were developed, which eventually led to an understanding of their medicinal uses—the science known as Ayurveda. It was also discovered that certain combinations of foods and spices create a balance and eliminate unpleasant effects, and so a dietary approach to health was established. Long before Hippocrates said, in 330 BC, "Let food be thy medicine," Vedic philosophy quite simply stated, "You are what you eat."

After I left the Taj group I planned to emigrate to Australia, but an old friend asked me to help him run a restaurant in London instead. Somehow London felt like home. There seemed to be tremendous opportunites for chefs - and room for a new style of Indian restaurant. In 1991 I became executive chef at the Namaste restaurant, and then in 1995 I opened the first Café Spice Namaste with my business partner Michael Gottlieb. We wanted the restaurant to reflect India's true nature: bright, vibrant, colorful, creative and above all diverse. India is often described as a nation that embodies unity in its diversity. It is a harmonious fusion of cultures, religions, languages and people from all walks of life. The philosophy behind our restaurant is to let customers experience that variety through the food of the subcontinent, and we always feature authentic regional dishes on the menu—especially those of Goa and the Parsee community, my two main culinary influences. We pride ourselves on creating a friendly and welcoming atmosphere. (*Namaste*, incidentally, means a gracious hello and welcome.)

Although Indian restaurants are extraordinarily popular outside India, the complexity of the cooking (and the unfamiliarity of some of the ingredients) deters many people from trying it at home. However, most of the recipes in this book are quite simple to prepare. If you prefer, use them as a guide and adjust them to suit your own tastes as you go along. That is the best way to learn about food, and Indian dishes vary from household to household in any case. Don't be afraid of making mistakes: these are easygoing, forgiving dishes that can easily be put right with a little bit of imagination. Very few of them require the precision that you would need to make a soufflé, for example. What is important is to taste as you go along, paying particular attention to the balance of flavors.

Planning an Indian meal is not as complex as some people fear, as long as you ensure that the food is well balanced. A creamy dish should be accompanied by light vegetables, preferably greens. Rice or whole wheat breads are generally preferable to heavier, richer breads (although Parsees or staunch Muslims may think otherwise). Always serve a fried dish with curry and rice and a good *cachumber* or salad with plenty of sliced onions to help digestion. In India pickles and *papads* are traditionally eaten with the main course, rather than as an appetizer. Make a habit of this when having an Indian meal and you will find that you relish the food much more.

These are just a few guidelines. With practice you will find that putting together a menu comes easily. If you are relaxed about the planning and keep it simple, you can't go wrong.

Starters, Snacks
and Finger Foods

Badal Jaam

EGGPLANT SLICES WITH TOMATO SAUCE AND A TANGY YOGURT DRESSING

Heat a few tablespoons of the oil in a heavy-bottomed frying pan and fry the eggplant slices (in batches if necessary) until well browned on both sides. Arrange them on a baking sheet without overlapping.

Give the tomatoes a quick whirl in a blender until roughly chopped. If using canned tomatoes, drain and mash coarsely with a potato masher to make a thick, spreadable sauce.

Heat the remaining oil in the pan in which the eggplants were fried. Add the onion and fry until light brown. Stir in the ginger and garlic (keeping aside a teaspoon of the garlic for the dressing) and fry until golden. Then add the ground chili, tomatoes and some salt and simmer until the mixture has a thick, saucelike consistency. Stir in half the cilantro, check the seasoning and add a sprinkling of fenugreek if you like.

Sprinkle *chaat masala* on the eggplant slices and spoon tomato sauce on each one. Cover with aluminum foil and place in an oven preheated to 275°F for 5-10 minutes, until heated through. Meanwhile, make the topping: whisk the yogurt until smooth. Stir in the reserved garlic, the remaining cilantro and the lemon juice.

Transfer the eggplant slices to a serving platter and top each one with a dollop of the yogurt dressing.

VARIATION
You can sprinkle on top some deep-fried egg noodles or *sev*. You can even top it with *chewda*, also known as Bombay mix.

TO TOAST FENUGREEK
This improves and mellows the flavor of dried fenugreek. Preheat the oven to 200°F. Spread out a packet of dried fenugreek leaves on a baking sheet, put them in the oven and then switch off the oven. Leave for 4-5 hours. The fenugreek will become lightly toasted. Pick out the stems, then crumble the fenugreek finely between your fingers. You could also try toasting it in an oven. Use as desired and store in an airtight jar for future use.

5-6 tbsp oil

2 long Asian eggplants or 1 globe eggplant, cut into rounds $\frac{1}{4}$-in thick

1 lb tomatoes (or 14-oz can of tomatoes)

1 onion, finely chopped

$\frac{3}{4}$-in piece of fresh ginger, finely chopped

8-10 garlic cloves, finely chopped

$\frac{1}{2}$ tsp ground dried red chili

2 tbsp chopped fresh cilantro

toasted fenugreek leaves (see below), to taste (optional)

chaat masala, for sprinkling

16 oz Greek-style yogurt

1 tbsp lemon juice

salt

Perhaps the most popular Indian snack in the west and also the most misunderstood. The product available in western markets and supermarkets does not even vaguely resemble the *bhajia* that would be made in an Indian home. Try this recipe. It is very simple and the results will astound you.

Onion Bhajia

MAKES 12-14

2 onions, sliced as thinly as possible

2 hot green chilies, finely chopped

½ tsp ground dried red chili

2 tbsp chopped fresh cilantro

½ tsp lemon juice

1 tsp cumin seeds, crushed

½ tsp ajwain (carom seeds), crushed

6-7 tbsp besan (chickpea flour)

½ tsp salt, or to taste

oil for deep-frying

2 tbsp water

Put the onions in a large bowl and add the green chilies, ground chili, fresh cilantro, lemon juice, cumin and *ajwain*. Sift the chickpea flour with the salt.

Heat plenty of oil in a *kadhai*-type container or a deep pan but do not let it get too hot.

Gradually add the sifted flour to the onion mixture, rubbing it in with your fingers until firm and sticky. Add the water and mix well. With your already messy fingers, put small dollops of the mixture into the oil to fry - just a few at a time or they will be soggy. The *bhajia* should be no bigger than 1 in. Fry them slowly until crisp and golden on the outside and cooked through in the center - about 3-4 minutes. If the oil is too hot they will be raw and gooey inside.

Drain in a sieve placed over a bowl and then serve immediately, with Green Chutney (see page 25), Green Coconut Chutney (see page 36) or Fresh Tomato Chutney (see page 119).

BHAJEE (BHAJI) AND BHAJIA - WHAT IS THE DIFFERENCE?
In restaurants and markets outside India these terms are used almost interchangeably, but in fact they refer to two very different dishes and should not be confused. A *bhajee* (or *bhaji*) is vegetables cooked in a sauce, whereas a *bhajia* is a fritter.

This can be garnished with hard-boiled eggs or olives, if you like.

Shinanio Chi Salade

MUSSEL COCKTAIL

Scrub the mussels well under cold running water and pull out the beards. Discard any open mussels that do not close when tapped on a work surface.

Heat the oil in a large pan, add the onion or shallots, garlic and carrot and fry gently until the onion is translucent. Increase the heat to high, add the mussels and green chili and sauté for 2–3 minutes. Now add the wine and some salt. Cover the pan and cook until the shells have opened. This should not take more than 2 minutes or so. Remove from the heat and let cool in the pan.

Remove the mussels from the pan, scraping any of the chopped ingredients back into the pan. Discard any mussels whose shells have not opened. Remove the meat from the shells and either discard the shells or keep the lower half of each shell if you want to present the mussels in them. Cover the mussels tightly when cool and keep them in the refrigerator until ready to serve.

Discard the chili. Reheat the vegetable mixture in the pan and simmer it until the liquid has evaporated. Let cool and then stir it into the mayonnaise, with the paprika, a little at a time until you are happy with the flavor. Mix in the cilantro and your dressing is ready.

Fold the mussels into the dressing. Now you can either shred the lettuce leaves and mix them with the mussels to make a cocktail, spoon each mussel into a half shell or arrange the mussels on a bed of lettuce.

24 medium or 36 small mussels

1 tbsp olive oil

1 onion or 4–5 shallots, finely chopped

2–3 garlic cloves, finely chopped

1 small carrot, finely diced or chopped

1 large green chili, slit open and seeded

$\frac{1}{2}$ glass of dry white wine

2 heaping tbsp mayonnaise (preferably homemade, see page 113)

$\frac{1}{4}$–$\frac{1}{2}$ tsp paprika

2 tsp chopped fresh cilantro

mixed lettuce leaves, for serving

salt

This recipe is very versatile. You can substitute oysters, mussels or any other shellfish for the scallops, or even a firm-fleshed fish such as monkfish, shark, tuna or swordfish. The mixture can also be used as a delicious omelet filling.

Adrak Lehsun Aur Mirch Kay Scallop

SCALLOPS WITH GINGER, GARLIC AND CHILI

20-30 fresh bay scallops

1 tbsp oil

1 tbsp finely chopped fresh ginger

6 garlic cloves, finely chopped

1-2 hot green chilies, chopped

½ tsp ground cumin

½ tsp ground coriander

½ tsp ground turmeric

½ tbsp finely chopped fresh cilantro

salt

Drain the scallops and leave them in the colander or sieve until you are ready to cook them.

Heat the oil in a heavy-bottomed frying pan until it is almost at smoking point. Put in the scallops and spread them out evenly. Immediately add the ginger, garlic and chilies. Toss and level out again. Don't stir, as this will reduce the temperature in the pan, causing the scallops to give off their juices and become rubbery.

Toss again and add the ground spices. Stir briefly to mix everything, then taste and add salt if necessary. Toss in the fresh cilantro.

The scallops should be cooked for no longer than 3-4 minutes; I prefer them cooked for only 2 minutes.

Serve immediately with the juices that the scallops will now have given off. Toasted brioche and green salad make good accompaniments.

TIP
Cilantro is a delicate herb that must be chopped carefully with a very sharp knife. If you go over it repeatedly with the knife, as for chopping parsley, it will bruise and turn black.

A simple yet delicious chicken dish. It can be made in minutes and will delight your guests. Shrimp, mussels, baby corn and slender green beans can all be substituted for the chicken. Adjust the cooking time as necessary but remember that the minimum of cooking will yield the best results.

Jeera Murg

CHICKEN WITH CUMIN

9 oz boneless chicken, cut into ½-in dice

1 tsp lemon juice

1-1½ tbsp oil

2 tsp cumin seeds, roasted and lightly crushed (see below)

2 tsp chopped fresh cilantro

salt

Sprinkle the chicken with the lemon juice and some salt. Heat the oil in a heavy-bottomed frying pan until it almost reaches smoking point, then put in the chicken and crushed cumin. Keep the flame high and swirl the chicken around, but not too often. This cools the pan down a little and allows the moisture from the chicken to escape. Toss for 2–3 minutes, until the chicken is cooked through, then taste and add more salt if necessary. Sprinkle with the cilantro and serve.

TO ROAST CUMIN OR CORIANDER SEEDS
Put the seeds in a heavy-bottomed frying pan and set the pan over low heat. Keep shaking the pan until the seeds are well roasted but not burnt. Crush them lightly in a mortar and pestle. They keep very well in a tightly sealed jar and can be used in many dishes.
Roasted crushed cumin is excellent for heartburn or an acidic stomach. Just chew some with a little sugar.

This method of cooking game birds was a particular favorite of the Maharanas of Oudh, better known as Avadh. Boned quails are available now from specialty butchers and some supermarkets.

Dudhia Bataer

QUAILS FRIED IN MILK BATTER

Put the milk in a deep pan and add the peppercorns, fennel, cardamom pods, bay leaves, saffron, cinnamon and some salt. Bring to a boil, add the quails, then reduce the heat and simmer until tender – about 8 minutes. Remove the quails from the pan and let cool. Simmer the milk until reduced to about 5 fl oz. Strain, discarding the spices, and let cool. Do not worry if the milk separates. The reduction will have a good flavor.

For the batter, put all the ingredients in a bowl and whisk together with enough of the reduced milk to give a fairly thick consistency.

Heat some *ghee* or oil for deep-frying. Cut the quails in half lengthwise and check the seasoning. Dip each quail half into the batter and fry briefly until golden brown. Do not allow them to brown too much or they will become tough. Drain on paper towels and serve immediately, with a salad.

You may like to serve Green Chutney (see page 25) or Fresh Tomato Chutney (see page 119) along with it.

SERVES 6

2 cups milk

5-6 black peppercorns, roughly crushed

1 tsp fennel seeds

6-8 green cardamom pods

1-2 bay leaves

a few saffron strands (use only good Mancha or pure Kashmiri saffron)

¾-in piece of cinnamon stick

6 boned quails

ghee or oil for deep-frying

salt

For the batter:

2 oz besan (chickpea flour)

¼ tsp ground fennel seed

¼ tsp ground dried red chili

1 tsp sugar

1 tbsp lemon juice

a few saffron strands

1 egg (optional – it gives a lighter batter)

salt

Liver is treated as a delicacy in India. This simple recipe uses plenty of fresh cilantro and mint, which really enhances the flavor of chicken livers. Serve with soft scrambled eggs and toast or with hot *chapatis*. Lamb's or calf's liver can be cooked in the same way but should be finely diced first.

Masala Ma Tatraveli Kaleji

SAUTÉED CHICKEN LIVERS WITH CILANTRO AND MINT

9 oz chicken livers

¾-in piece of fresh ginger, very finely chopped

6 garlic cloves, very finely chopped

1 large hot green chili, very finely chopped

¼ tsp ground turmeric

½ tsp ground cumin

juice of ½ lemon

2 tbsp oil

2½ tbsp chopped fresh cilantro

1½ tbsp chopped fresh mint

salt

Clean the chicken livers and cut them in half. Mix together the ginger, garlic, chili, turmeric, cumin, lemon juice and some salt and then stir this mixture into the chicken livers until they are thoroughly coated.

Heat the oil to smoking point in a large heavy-bottomed frying pan, then add the livers. Don't stir them too much; just shake the pan to toss them or stir very lightly with a wooden spatula. Cook for 4–5 minutes, until browned on the outside but still pink inside, or longer if you prefer them well done. Toss in the cilantro and mint, then check the seasoning, adding a squeeze of lemon juice if you like, and serve immediately.

Idlis are one of India's greatest snack or breakfast foods. Though southern Indian in origin, they have become popular throughout the country. The traditional recipe takes 24 hours to make but here is a quick and easy version - a specialty of my wife, Pervin. If you don't have an *idli* dish (available from southern Indian markets) for steaming the cakes you can improvise with an ordinary cake pan, although the *idli* will not be as light.

Instant Rava Idli

INSTANT SEMOLINA CAKES

Mix the semolina and yogurt together, then stir in the green onion, tomato, chilies and cilantro.

Heat the oil in a small frying pan until very hot. Add one or two mustard seeds to check that the oil is hot enough: they should crackle. Add all the mustard seeds, then when they start to crackle, add the curry leaves and lastly the asafetida. Remove from the heat, cool slightly, then pour into the yogurt and semolina mixture straight from the pan. Stir in the fruit salts.

If you are using an *idli* steamer, grease the dish with oil or butter and bring about ¾ cm of water to a boil in the pan. Pour in the batter, up to the top of each small mold, and steam for about 10 minutes, until the mixture feels spongy and doesn't stick to your fingers.

If you don't have an *idli* steamer, pour all the batter into a greased shallow cake pan and steam it in an ordinary steamer for about 20 minutes. Cut into wedges to serve.

Once unmolded, the *idli* can be kept warm wrapped in a cloth. They can also be reheated by steaming again if necessary, enclosed, or wrapped loosely in a cloth.

6 oz semolina

⅔ cup yogurt

1 green onion, finely chopped

1 tomato, seeded and finely chopped

2 hot green chilies, finely chopped

1 tbsp chopped fresh cilantro

2 tbsp oil

½ tsp mustard seeds

2-4 curry leaves, finely shredded

a large pinch of asafetida

1 tsp fruit salts (such as Eno's or Andrew's)

VARIATION
The *idli* can be stuffed with left-over cooked ground beef or Green Coconut Chutney (see page 36) for an inventive variation. Pour half the mixture into the dish or mold, add the filling, then cover with the remaining mixture and steam as usual.

This stuffed, rolled *chapati* used to be Bombay's best-selling street snack until it was overtaken by modern American-style fast food. However, it is still a favorite with many.

Frankie

MAKES 8

3 eggs

dried ground red chili (optional)

oil, ghee or butter for frying

8 plain chapatis or flour tortillas

2 onions, sliced

1 tbsp chopped fresh cilantro

10 mint leaves, coarsely chopped

salt

For the filling:

2 tbsp oil

1 lb boned leg of lamb, cut into ½-in dice

2 onions, very finely chopped

2 tbsp Ginger/Garlic Paste (see page 61)

1 tbsp ground coriander

1 tsp ground cumin

1 tbsp red chili paste (see below)

4-5 tbsp Greek-style yogurt

1-2 tomatoes, chopped (optional)

1 tbsp lemon juice

1 tsp garam masala (see page 123)

2 tbsp chopped fresh cilantro

1 tbsp chopped fresh mint

salt

To make the filling, heat the oil in a casserole, add the lamb and cook over medium-high heat until the meat is browned and any liquid has dried out. Add the onions, ginger/garlic paste, coriander, cumin and chili paste. Sauté until the onions and spices start to turn a rich, dark color, stirring and scraping the bottom of the pan frequently. Season with salt, then reduce the heat, cover and cook for 15-20 minutes, stirring frequently to prevent sticking. If the mixture dries out too quickly, stir in a couple of tablespoons of water.

Stir in the yogurt and the tomatoes, if using, then cover and continue to cook until the lamb is tender and a thick, rich-looking sauce has formed. Add the lemon juice, *garam masala*, cilantro and mint, then cover and set aside. If necessary, remove any excess oil floating on the top (save it to use in other lamb dishes).

Beat the eggs well with 3 tablespoons of water. Add salt and, if you like, some ground chili. Heat a *tawa* or griddle over medium heat. Coat it with a teaspoon of oil or brush with a little *ghee* or butter. Put a *chapati* or flour tortilla on the pan and pour a little egg on the top, spreading it over the bread with the back of a spoon. As soon as the egg coagulates, flip the bread over and coat the other side. When both sides are golden brown, remove from the pan. Place a tablespoon or two of the lamb mixture on top, sprinkle with sliced onion, chopped cilantro and mint, then roll up and serve. Repeat with the remaining *chapatis* or tortillas.

TIP

To make your own red chili paste, snip a handful of red chilies into pieces, then soak in about 5 fl oz water until swollen and soft. Purée in a blender with the soaking liquid to make a thick paste. Store in the refrigerator.

I was taught to prepare these by the mother of the managing director of the Taj hotel group. Serve with a fresh green chutney, such as the one on page 25 or page 36, or tomato ketchup spiced up with some chopped green chili and a little chopped fresh cilantro. Spring roll pastry is available in most Asian markets. If you cannot get it you could substitute filo dough, although this absorbs more oil when fried.

Goan Shrimp Samosas

Wash the shrimp and drain well, ensuring there is no moisture left. Chop them very finely. Pound the cumin and coriander seeds to a coarse powder in a mortar and pestle. Heat the oil in a pan and sauté the chopped onions until softened, then add the ginger, garlic and green chilies. Add the cumin and coriander, stir for a minute or two, then increase the heat to high and add the shrimp. Stir well to break up lumps and cook for 2-3 minutes, until any liquid has evaporated. Season with salt to taste and stir in the lemon juice and chopped cilantro. Transfer the mixture to a plate and let cool.

Place a 9-in plate upside down over the pile of spring roll pastry sheets and cut round it with a knife to give 8 circles of pastry. (Either discard the trimmings or cut them into small pieces and deep-fry them later for a delightful snack when mixed with a salad - see *Chaats*, pages 30-31). Cut the stack of dough rounds in half to make semicircles, then peel off the sheets in pairs. Keep them covered with a cloth while you make the samosas or they will become dry and brittle.

Take one of the double-thickness semicircles and fold over one-third, then apply beaten egg or flour and water paste along the edge to seal. Fold over the other third to form a cone and seal the edge again. Open up the top and put in just over a tablespoon of the filling. Seal the opening with the egg or paste and press well together, ensuring that there are no gaps. Sometimes there is a little hole at the bottom tip, so seal this if necessary. Prepare the remaining samosas in the same way.

Heat some oil in a large pan and deep-fry the samosas over medium heat for 2-3 minutes or until golden. Drain on paper towels and serve.

MAKES 8

10 oz shelled raw shrimp

1 tsp cumin seeds

1 tsp coriander seeds

4 tbsp oil

2 onions, very finely chopped

3/4-in piece of fresh ginger, very finely chopped

6-8 garlic cloves, very finely chopped

3-4 hot green chilies (seeded if you like), very finely chopped

1 1/2 tsp lemon juice

2-3 tbsp chopped fresh cilantro

8 large sheets of spring roll pastry

beaten egg or flour and water paste, to seal

oil for deep-frying

salt

The *tamota ni gravy*, or tomato sauce, keeps well, covered, in the refrigerator and is excellent with croquettes, fried fish or chicken. For extra flavor you can include fresh green chilies, slit open lengthwise (otherwise they might explode in the pan), and a few cloves, putting them in with the dried red chilies.

Machchi Na Pattice
Nay Tamota Ni Gravy

For the sauce:

2-3 tbsp oil

2 pieces of cinnamon stick

2 large dried red chilies, broken into 3-4 pieces each

2 small to medium onions, finely chopped

1 heaping tbsp Ginger/Garlic Paste (see page 61)

5 tomatoes, chopped, or 14 oz-can of chopped tomatoes

1 tbsp malt vinegar

1 tbsp grated jaggery

1½ tsp prepared tamarind pulp (see page 28) or paste, or ½ tsp concentrate (optional)

salt

For the fish cakes:

8 oz white fish fillets, skinned

1 large green chili, chopped

¾-in piece of fresh ginger, chopped

6-8 garlic cloves, chopped

2 tbsp chopped fresh cilantro

1 tsp salt

1 tbsp lemon juice

1 egg

2 slices of white bread, soaked in water for a few seconds, then squeezed out thoroughly

For frying the fish cakes:

4 oz all-purpose flour

2-3 eggs

oil

FISH CAKES WITH TOMATO SAUCE

First make the sauce. Heat the oil in a saucepan, add the cinnamon sticks and sauté until swollen and deep brown in color but not burnt. Add the chilies and cook for 15-20 seconds, then add the onions. Sauté until they are softened but not browned. Add the ginger/garlic paste and sauté for another minute or so, then stir in the tomatoes. Add the vinegar, jaggery and tamarind, if using, then cover and simmer for 15-20 minutes, stirring occasionally, until thick and saucelike. Taste and add salt if necessary.

Next prepare the fish cakes. Put all the ingredients in a food processor and process until well combined. Taste and add more salt if necessary. (If you prefer not to taste the raw mixture, fry a small piece and taste it. Don't make the fish cakes until you have approved the taste for yourself.) Divide the mixture into 8 balls. Spread the flour out in a baking sheet big enough to hold all the fish cakes. Beat the eggs thoroughly in a shallow bowl or soup plate. Pour enough oil into a frying pan to fill it to a depth of about ¼ inch and set it over medium heat. Flatten each ball to about ½ inch thick, smoothing the edges so that they are not jagged or uneven. Dip each fish cake into the flour, then into the egg, allowing excess egg to run off, and then place in the hot oil. Raise the heat if the oil begins to foam. If you want the fish cakes to have a frilly appearance, make sure the eggs are well beaten and fry the fish cakes immediately. Fry for a few minutes, turning once, until golden brown on both sides, then transfer to a baking sheet lined with paper towels to drain.

Serve with the tomato sauce. The fish cakes can also be eaten cold, stuffed in small bread rolls as a snack.

A simple yet surprisingly variable egg dish. My mother taught me to make it and she makes the best I have ever had. Serve with mango chutney and soft bread. In India we have gorgeous breads. One of the most common is *ladi pao*, meaning tray bread. This is similar to dinner rolls but, unlike the ones available in England, contains no preservatives or improvers, which make the bread unnaturally light. A rustic country bread or warm baguette is also good with this dish.

Papeta Pur Eeda

EGGS ON POTATOES

2-3 tbsp oil

1 tsp cumin seeds

1 small hot green chili, finely chopped

2 garlic cloves, finely chopped

1 onion, finely sliced

1 large potato, peeled and cut into slices about 1/8 in thick

1 tbsp finely chopped fresh cilantro

4 eggs

salt

Heat the oil in a large frying pan, add the cumin seeds and allow them to sizzle for a minute. Add the green chili and garlic and sauté for a minute or two. Add the onion and sauté for a few minutes, until translucent, then add the potato slices. Cook for 3-4 minutes, without letting them brown, then sprinkle with salt and level out the mixture. Pour in enough water to come just below the contents of the pan, cover and cook over low heat until the potato is tender but not mushy. Sprinkle with the cilantro, check the seasoning, then mix gently by folding everything in a slow motion and leveling it out again.

Make sure the sides of the pan are clean. Use an egg to make 4 indentations in the mixture, well spaced out. They should be roughly $1\frac{1}{2}$ in from the side of the pan. Break an egg into each indentation, making sure the yolk goes in it, then cover the pan and cook on very low heat. The eggs will poach in the steam.

When done to your liking, (I prefer my yolk soft), cut into 4 segments and serve with mango chutney and bread.

Papeta Na Pattice

POTATO CAKES

2 large floury potatoes (weighing about 1 lb in total), peeled and chopped

1 tbsp chopped fresh cilantro

1-2 green chilies, finely chopped

1 tsp chaat masala

1/2 tsp ground cumin

1 tsp lemon juice

1 tsp salt, or to taste

cornstarch

oil for frying

a little sugar

Boil the potatoes until tender. Drain well and return the pan to very low heat. Dry the potato out in the pan by stirring continuously with a wooden spoon, scraping the bottom of the pan. After all that stirring the potatoes probably won't need mashing; just break up any lumps that remain.

Mix the potatoes with the cilantro, chilies, *chaat masala*, cumin, lemon juice and salt, working the mixture to a pliable dough with your hands. If it seems too moist, add some cornstarch until it is dry enough not to stick to your palms. Check the seasoning and then divide the mixture into balls about 1 1/2 inch in diameter. If you have kneaded the dough well the balls should have a smooth edge and will not crack when flattened. If they do crack, smooth the edges.

Pour some oil into a large frying pan to a depth of about 1/2 in and set it over medium heat. Spread some cornstarch on a large plate and roll the potato balls in it to coat. Flatten them to about 1/2 in thick, shake off excess cornstarch and fry them in the hot oil until well browned. Remove from the pan and drain on paper towels.

Serve in one of the following suggested ways: with a Raita (see page 118); with a simple Ragda (see page 104) and small bread rolls; with a chutney such as Tamarind and Date Chutney (see opposite) for a quick snack; or with tomato ketchup that has chopped chili, garlic and fresh cilantro stirred into it.

VARIATIONS

• Roll the pattice in finely chopped peanuts or cashew nuts instead of cornstarch. This will give a nice nutty flavor and is more interesting, but do make sure that none of your guests is allergic to nuts.

• Stuff the pattice with nuts, green chutney, green peas, grated paneer, cottage cheese, ricotta or sautéed shrimp - try the filling for Goan Shrimp Samosas on page 19.

This is one of Bombay's all-time-great snacks, and thousands of portions are sold there daily. If you have everything ready in advance it can be assembled in a matter of minutes. The chutneys keep well in a sealed jar in the refrigerator so it is worth making up a large amount.

Sev Batata Poorie

CRISPY POORIE WITH CHICKPEA VERMICELLI AND POTATOES

To make the *poorie*, sift the whole wheat flour, rice flour and salt into a bowl, then stir in the semolina. Warm the oil slightly, then stir it into the mixture. Gradually add enough water to make a firm dough (about the same consistency as pasta dough). Knead until smooth, then cover and set aside for an hour.

Meanwhile, prepare the chutneys. For the tamarind chutney, bring 7 oz water to a boil in a saucepan, then add the tamarind, dates and jaggery and simmer for about 20 minutes, until the dates are soft. Let cool, then purée and season to taste with salt.

For the green chutney, just purée all the ingredients in a blender, adding enough water to make a thick paste. Check the seasoning, adding a little more sugar if necessary.

Divide the *poorie* dough into 4 pieces and roll out each piece very thinly – it should be a little less than ⅛ in thick. Cut out rounds with a 1½ in pastry cutter. Pour some oil into a *karahi* or wok to a depth of about 1 in and place over medium heat (if it is too hot the dough will puff, which is not ideal for this recipe). Fry the *poorie*, a few at a time, for ½–1 minute, until golden brown. They will sink to the bottom of the oil at first, then rise to the top when they are about done. Drain well and let cool.

To assemble everything, place 12 *poorie* on a platter (any extra ones can be stored in an airtight container lined with paper towels). Top them with the potato, then the onion and then the cilantro. Sprinkle with *chaat masala*. Top each *poorie* with the chutneys – about a teaspoon of each or a bit less. Next sprinkle the *sev* and cilantro on top. Serve immediately.

8 oz whole wheat flour

2 oz rice flour

1 tsp salt

2 oz semolina

4 tbsp oil, plus oil for frying

sev and chopped fresh cilantro, to garnish

For the tamarind and date chutney:

1 tbsp tamarind concentrate or 2 tbsp tamarind paste

8-10 dates, stoned

1 oz jaggery

salt

For the green chutney:

½ oz fresh mint leaves

½ oz fresh cilantro

3-4 green chilies

½ tsp salt

3-4 garlic cloves

1 tsp cumin seeds

2 tsp lemon juice

a little sugar

For the topping:

1 large potato, boiled and diced

1 onion, chopped

2 tbsp chopped fresh cilantro

chaat masala, for sprinkling

This is a Parsee specialty from Gujerat. Parsees love eggs and often include this type of omelet in their picnics or use it as a filling stuffed into *chapatis*. It is like a Spanish omelet except it has more spices and no potato.

Bhujelo Poro

BAKED SPICY OMELET

2 slender green chilies

3 garlic cloves

$1/2$–$3/4$-in piece of fresh ginger

1 tbsp chopped fresh cilantro

$1/2$ tsp cumin seeds

$1/4$ tsp salt

a pinch of ground turmeric

2 egg yolks

4 egg whites

1 tsp all-purpose flour

1 tsp ghee or clarified butter

Put the chilies, garlic, ginger, coriander, cumin, salt and turmeric in a mortar and grind to a fine paste (or use a blender, adding a very little water if necessary). Lightly beat the egg yolks, then stir in the spice paste. Beat the egg whites until stiff, then gently fold in the egg yolk mixture and the flour.

Heat the *ghee* or clarified butter in an 8-in ovenproof frying pan until very hot. Add the omelet mixture and leave on the heat for a few seconds, then transfer the pan to the center of an oven preheated to 425°F and bake until the omelet is well risen, light and fluffy. It shouldn't take longer than 5 minutes. Serve immediately, with warm bread or toast and a sweet chutney.

TIP
When selecting fresh ginger, look for a smooth piece with as few knots as possible.

This is another Parsee specialty and, like several of their dishes, was probably created centuries ago. It is perhaps the most tedious method of cooking scrambled eggs ever invented, but I think it is the very best. However, patience is essential.

I would like to make a suggestion that I find very effective (although my mother may not agree). The mixture without the eggs and butter can be kept covered in the refrigerator for months. You can then use it as you wish, adding just one egg or two if you like, and finishing it off with the fresh cilantro. It also makes an excellent omelet.

Akoori

SPICY SCRAMBLED EGGS

Heat the oil in a pan and fry the sliced onions in it until crisp and golden (see page 103). Drain and let dry on paper towels.

Put half the oil back in the pan and reheat gently. Add the ginger, garlic and green chili and fry until the garlic is golden. Add all the ground spices and continue to cook gently for a minute or two. Add the tomato, stir for a minute and then return the onions to the pan. Add the raisins, if using (the Parsees of Bharooch in Gujerat love it made with golden raisins).

Now stir in the vinegar, lemon juice, sugar and some salt to taste. Remove from the heat and drain off as much oil as you can (save the oil, as it is good to use in other dishes). Add the butter and eggs and beat them into the mixture. Return to very low heat and cook very slowly, stirring continuously, to achieve a creamy, scrambled texture. Add the fresh cilantro and check the seasoning. Serve with toast or warm bread.

6 tbsp oil

2 onions, finely sliced

$^3/_4$-in piece of fresh ginger, finely chopped

4 garlic cloves, finely chopped

1 green chili, finely chopped

$^3/_4$ tsp ground cumin

1 tsp ground coriander

a large pinch of ground turmeric

$^1/_2$ tsp ground red dried chili

1 tomato, seeded and chopped

1 tbsp golden raisins (optional)

1 tsp malt vinegar

$^1/_2$ tsp lemon juice

1 tsp sugar

$^1/_2$ oz butter

6 large eggs

1-2 tbsp chopped fresh cilantro

salt

A Maharashtrian salad from the Ratnagiri district, which is on India's west coast, south of Bombay. Roasted salted cashew nuts or almonds can be substituted for the peanuts. A few diced olives can be added to the salad, although this is not authentically Indian.

Tantia Ani Shingdaney Chi Usli

EGG AND PEANUT SALAD

5 eggs

6 tablespoons fresh or thawed frozen grated coconut (see page 96)

1-2 large hot green chilies, finely chopped

2 tbsp finely chopped fresh cilantro

1 tbsp prepared tamarind pulp (see below) or paste, or 1½ tsp concentrate

3-4 tablespoons roasted peanuts, coarsely chopped

salt

Optional extras:

1 tbsp chopped shallots

2 tbsp chopped tomatoes

Hard-boil the eggs by immersing them in boiling water and simmering for 7 minutes. Remove from the heat and cool them in the water by adding a few ice cubes to it. This cools them slowly and ensures that they are cooked through.

Shell the eggs and take out the yolks. Cut the whites into small dice and crumble the yolks roughly with a fork. Mix in all the other ingredients and season to taste. If you are serving the salad immediately, include the shallots and tomatoes.

VARIATION
Flakes of tuna, or *boogdi* as it is known in Goa, make an excellent addition. You can also mix in or serve with lettuce if you like.

TO PREPARE TAMARIND PULP
Ready-to-use tamarind paste and concentrate are now available in Indian markets and some supermarkets. If using concentrate, you will need to dilute it with water before use.

Tamarind is also available as a compressed block containing the seeds and pulp. To prepare this, soak the block in about 17 fl oz boiling water for at least 1 hour. Then mash it with your fingers, squeezing out all the pulp from the seeds, and pass it through a sieve, rubbing it through with a spoon. Discard the seeds and fibers left in the sieve and use the pulp as required. It can be stored in a jar in the refrigerator for some time.

Chaats

Chaat means 'lick' in Hindi, Gujerati and a few other Indian languages. *Chaats* are basically cold finger foods or light salads, whose ingredients vary according to the time of year. They are simple to make and you need only a few ingredients unless you are going for something complicated. The essential seasoning is *chaat masala*, which always contains *amchur* (mango powder), *jeera* (ground cumin) and *kala namak* (black salt). Other ingredients for the *masala* vary, although red chili is the most common. Your best bet is to buy packets of ready-made *chaat masala*.

Aloo Chaat

POTATO SALAD

1 large or 2 medium potatoes, boiled, peeled and cut into small dice

1 small onion, chopped

1 green chili, seeded and chopped

1 tbsp chopped fresh cilantro

1 plum tomato, chopped

1 tsp chaat masala, or to taste

The best known of Indian *chaats*, this is very simple to make. Place all the ingredients in a bowl and toss lightly until well combined. Taste and add more *masala* if needed. Serve plain or with Yogurt, Tamarind and Chili Dip (see page 114).

VARIATIONS
• Add lettuce or diced fruit such as apple and banana.

• Lightly crush some crispy *poories* or deep-fried flour tortillas and stir them into the *chaat* just before serving.

• Mix with lettuce and cold chicken *tikka* or shrimp to make an excellent accompaniment, starter, or snack to serve with drinks.

• Channa Chaat: substitute chickpeas for the potatoes, or blend both together.

• Cashew Nut Chaat: substitute roasted cashews for the potatoes, or use half potatoes and half nuts. To roast your own cashews, put the nuts into a bowl, pour over boiling water and let soak for a minute or two. Drain through a sieve and let dry. Rub in 2 tsp oil for every 9 oz nuts, then sprinkle with 1 tsp salt per 9 oz, or to taste. Mix well. Spread out on a baking sheet and roast in an oven preheated to 325-350°F for 40-45 minutes. Stir the nuts regularly and do not let them brown too much. Switch off the oven and let the nuts cool in it. Store in an airtight jar for up to a month.

Hara Moong Aur Anar Ki Salaat

GREEN SPROUTED MUNG BEAN AND POMEGRANATE SALAD

Soak 4 oz green mung beans in water overnight, then drain and fold them into a clean towel. Dampen the towel and set it aside in a warm place in your kitchen. Keep the towel wet at all times. In 2-3 days you should have sprouts just big enough for the salad. Mix the sprouts with the ingredients for Aloo Chaat (see opposite), plus the seeds of 2 pomegranates.

I like to add 3-4 heaping tablespoons of corn to this *chaat*. It is delicious served in toasted pita bread with some soft cheese or *paneer.*

Fruit Chaat

In India fruit *chaats* are very popular in summer. Any diced fruit can be tossed with *chaat masala,* although bananas, apples, papayas, melons, pomegranates and oranges are especially good. Sometimes chopped fresh cilantro is added. Serve fruit *chaats* immediately.

Fish and Seafood

A classic recipe. When you want to have a great meal, serve this with my all-time favorite dish, Dhan Daar Nay Vaghaar (see page 103). Pacific pompano is the best fish to use, although rockfish and flounder are also good.

Masala Ma Tareli Machchi

PARSEE FISH FRIED IN MASALA

Rub the fish fillets with the turmeric and some salt and set aside for half an hour. Mix together all the remaining ingredients except the oil to make a paste, then taste and check the seasoning. Rub the paste onto the fish, then taste again, sprinkling on more lemon juice or salt if necessary. Place in the refrigerator if you are not cooking it immediately.

Heat a little oil in a large frying pan, add the fish and cook until well colored underneath before turning it over. Do not let the oil get too hot or the coating will burn very rapidly. When ready, the fish should be crisp outside and delicately soft inside.

about 14 oz white fish fillet, cut into 8 pieces about 4 in long

$\frac{1}{4}$ tsp ground turmeric

1 tbsp lemon juice

1 tsp ground red chili

1 tsp ground cumin

1 tsp ground coriander

$1\frac{1}{2}$ tsp Ginger/Garlic Paste (see page 61)

oil for shallow-frying

salt

VARIATION
After rubbing the paste onto the fish you can dust the fillets in flour, coat them in egg and then in semolina (or just dip them in egg). Deep-fry as you would a breaded fillet of fish.

A simple curry that does not need a great deal of preparation. Pacific pompano gives the best flavor but you could substitute other white fish fillets.

Leeli Machchi Ni Curry

GREEN FISH CURRY

2 tbsp oil
1 onion, finely sliced
6 garlic cloves, crushed
1½-in piece of fresh ginger, crushed
2 hot green chilies, seeded and finely chopped
½ tsp ground turmeric
14 fl oz can of coconut milk
4 green cardamom pods
4 cloves
5-6 curry leaves
¾-in piece of cinnamon stick
2 tbsp chopped fresh cilantro
4 large fish steaks
salt

Heat the oil in a large pan, add the onion and sauté for a few minutes, until translucent. Add the garlic, ginger and green chilies and cook for 2 minutes, taking care not to let them brown. Stir in the turmeric and cook for a few seconds, then pour in the coconut milk. Bring slowly to a boil, stirring right from the bottom of the mixture. Add some salt, then the cardamom, cloves, curry leaves and cinnamon. Simmer for a couple of minutes, until the mixture has thickened slightly, then add the cilantro and cook for another minute or two. Add the fish and cook for 2-4 minutes, depending on the thickness of the steaks, then cover the pan, remove from the heat and set aside for about 5 minutes. The fish will continue to cook in the heat of the curry. Serve with fried *papads* (*papadums*) and plain rice or a light *pulao*.

This traditional Parsee dish is very popular at weddings and on other festive occasions. Banana leaves are available in Thai markets and some Indian ones. If you cannot find them, substitute aluminum foil, although the flavor will not be the same. You can also use a whole fish instead of steaks if you prefer. The chutney is good in sandwiches and with a wide range of snacks.

Patrani Machchi

about 1½ lb Pacific pompano steaks, cut ¾ in thick (about 3 per person), or 4 halibut or other white fish steaks

½ tsp ground turmeric

salt

1 package banana leaves

malt vinegar for sprinkling

For the green coconut chutney:

9 oz fresh or thawed frozen grated coconut (see page 96) or 5 oz coconut powder

1 bunch of fresh cilantro (the large bunches available from Indian markets, not a supermarket bunch)

1 bunch of fresh mint (again, from Indian markets)

4-5 green chilies

6-8 garlic cloves

1 heaping tsp cumin seeds

1 tbsp sugar

juice of 1 large lime, or to taste

salt

FISH IN BANANA LEAF WITH GREEN COCONUT CHUTNEY

Rub the fish with the turmeric and some salt and set aside while you make the chutney. Put all the ingredients for the chutney in a blender and process to a thick paste, adding a little water if necessary. Taste and adjust the seasoning, adding more lime juice if you like. Coat the fish with the coconut chutney on both sides.

Remove the stems from the banana leaves and string the sides (just like stringing green beans). Cut them into squares big enough to wrap the fish steaks in. To make them supple, run each piece over a hot burner until it changes color and becomes soft. Do not overdo it; just passing it over the heat once on each side should be sufficient.

Wrap each piece of fish in a banana leaf and then tie with string (you can use the strings from the banana leaves).

Place the fish parcels on a baking sheet containing about ⅛ in water, sprinkle a little vinegar over them, and then place in an oven preheated to 375°F for 20 minutes. Remove the strings and serve the fish in the banana leaf.

Fish curry is synonymous with Goa. It is a staple part of the diet and the vast majority of Goans cannot do without it. Serve with Arborio or Camargue rice or with plain steamed long grain rice. It is also good eaten cold or slightly warm the next day, with ciabatta or any crusty bread.

Goan Fish Curry

1 lb Pacific pompano steaks or chunky pieces of fillet (or use other firm white fish)

¼ tsp ground turmeric

5 tbsp oil

1 onion, finely sliced

¾-in piece of fresh ginger, finely shredded

2 hot green chilies, finely shredded

10 fl oz water or fish stock

4 tbsp prepared tamarind pulp (see page 28) or paste, or 1½ tbsp concentrate

2-3 cokums (or 1 tart plum)

salt

For the masala:

2 oz dried red chilies (select large ones with a deep color)

2 tsp coriander seeds

1 tsp cumin seeds

6-8 garlic cloves

1½-in piece of fresh ginger

½ tsp ground turmeric

9 oz fresh or frozen grated coconut (see page 96) or 5 oz coconut powder

Put all the ingredients for the *masala* into a blender and mix to a smooth, thick paste, adding only enough water to process the mixture; it should not be runny.

Sprinkle the fish with the turmeric and some salt and set aside. Pour the oil into a large, heavy-bottomed pan and heat until it forms a haze, then add the onion, ginger and green chilies. Sauté until softened, then add the *masala* and cook, stirring frequently, until the oil begins to separate out from it.

Add the water or stock and bring to a boil, then stir in the tamarind and cokums. Simmer for 5 minutes or so, then check the consistency. It should be like a pouring sauce, so if it is too thin, simmer for a little longer. Taste and adjust the seasoning if necessary.

Now put the fish in and simmer over medium heat for 3-4 minutes without stirring. Remove from the heat, cover the pan and let sit for at least 5 minutes to allow the fish to cook in the heat of the sauce. In this way it will have a perfect texture and will not break up.

VARIATIONS
This curry is also suitable for shrimp, crab, lobster, mussels and even oysters. You can also use chicken (which will need sautéing separately first) or cauliflower and tomato with new potatoes. It is not suitable for red meats.

WHAT IS A *MASALA*?
A *masala* is a mixture of spices, seasonings and herbs, finely chopped or puréed together to form a savory paste that is used as the basis for a dish. It can be a simple combination such as ginger, garlic and cumin or something much more complex. A fresh chutney, such as the green chutney on page 25, is also known as a *masala*.

A popular recipe that varies from region to region and even from home to home. The best fish to use is Pacific pompano, available from Chinese fishmongers or frozen from Indian markets. Either serve one fish per person as a main course or serve it as the Goans would, with a chicken curry, rice and Cachumber (see page 60) - in which case it will serve 8.

Fish Recheade

GOAN STUFFED FISH

Scale the fish, wash well and dry on paper towels. You now need to bone each fish. With a sharp, thin knife, make a cut the length of the backbone, then, on each side, use the knife to ease the fillet away from the bones, right down to the stomach cavity. Do not slit the stomach cavity open. All you are doing is separating the flesh from the bones but not completely filleting the fish. Snip either end of the backbone with scissors, then remove the backbone and the entire skeleton with it. Take out the guts as well if the fish has not been gutted. Remove any stray bones. Clean the abdominal cavity and wash the fish inside. Allow to drain well or pat dry with paper towels. Sprinkle the lime juice and some salt inside each fish and set aside.

For the stuffing, heat the oil in a pan, add the curry leaves and onions and sauté until golden brown. Add the masala and cook for a few minutes until you see the oil just oozing out through it. Stir in the shrimp powder and some salt, then add the chopped cilantro. Remove from the heat and let cool. Check the seasoning and then apply the mixture inside the fish on either side. If possible, refrigerate the fish for a few hours before cooking. This will improve the flavor and the flesh will almost start to pickle, which greatly reduces the cooking time.

Heat some oil in a large frying pan set over medium heat. Cook the fish until well browned underneath, then turn and cook the other side.

Alternatively cook the fish under the broiler or on a barbecue. If broiling, brush the grill rack and the fish with oil. If barbecuing, place the fish on a piece of aluminum foil to prevent the skin from coming off, and brush the fish with oil before and during cooking.

4 x 1 lb white fish fillets

juice of 2 limes

oil for frying

salt

For the stuffing:

3 tbsp oil

15-20 curry leaves

4 onions, sliced

**4 tbsp Piri-piri Masala
(see page 123)**

4 tsp shrimp powder

4 tbsp chopped fresh cilantro

salt

A northern specialty, *tikka* is one of the best known of all Indian dishes. It is normally prepared with chicken but here monkfish makes an interesting alternative. If monkfish is not available, select a chunky fish such as grouper, red snapper, pike or cod. To make chicken *tikka*, simply substitute chicken for the monkfish.

Machli Kay Tikkay

MONKFISH TIKKA

14-oz monkfish fillet, cut into 1½-in cubes (tikkas)

8 garlic cloves

2-in piece of fresh ginger

¾ tsp cumin seeds

¾ tsp coriander seeds

¾ tsp ground dried red chili

½ tsp ground turmeric

½ tsp garam masala (see page 123)

2 tbsp lime juice

3½ tbsp mustard oil or peanut oil

7 oz Greek-style yogurt

melted butter for basting

salt and white pepper

Rub salt and pepper into the monkfish and set aside. Put the garlic, ginger, spices, lime juice, oil and half the yogurt into a blender and process to a smooth paste. When all the spices are well ground, transfer to a bowl and whisk in the remaining yogurt. Taste and check the seasoning, adding more chili if you wish. Mix in the fish cubes and check the seasoning again. Cover and refrigerate for at least 4 hours, preferably overnight.

Now cook the *tikka* either under a broiler or on a barbecue, basting well with melted butter and turning the pieces until cooked through. (Put the *tikka* on skewers, if you like, to make turning easier.) If broiling, place the fish on the broiler rack and make sure the heat is not too high. Alternatively, cook the fish in an oven preheated to 450°F for 8-10 minutes.

Dahi Maach

BENGALI FISH CURRY

1 lb bass or Pacific pompano, cut
into large chunks

½ tsp ground turmeric

4 tbsp mustard oil or ghee

¾-in piece of fresh
ginger, crushed

5-6 garlic cloves, crushed

3 onions, very finely chopped

4-5 large dried red chilies,
snipped into tiny pieces

9 oz thick yogurt

3 bay leaves

2 green cardamom pods

1 tsp sugar

½ tsp garam masala
(see page 123)

salt

Rub the fish with the turmeric and some salt and set aside for an hour or two. Drain well, reserving the juices, then rinse thoroughly and pat dry.

Heat the mustard oil or *ghee* in a large frying pan, add the fish and fry for about 2 minutes, just to seal. Do not allow it to color. Remove the fish from the pan.

Mix the ginger, garlic, onions and chilies into the yogurt and beat well. Transfer the mustard oil or *ghee* to a large saucepan and reheat. Add the yogurt mixture and bring slowly to a boil. Add the bay leaves and cardamom and then the fish. Sprinkle in the sugar and *garam masala*. Pour in the reserved juices from the fish and bring to a simmer. Cover the pan, remove from the heat and let sit for 5-7 minutes to allow the fish to cook through in the heat of the sauce. Check the seasoning, then serve with plain rice and mango pickle.

VERSATILE TURMERIC
You may wonder why I often toss turmeric into my recipes. There are several reasons but the most important are that it has antiseptic qualities, which help to kill bacteria; it is an excellent coagulant, so it prevents too much liquid seeping out; and it acts as a preservative.

Turmeric is so useful that in several remote areas of India it is carried in trucks and cars on long journeys. This is not only for its medicinal properties but also to help mend burst radiators. If, for instance, a buffalo hits the car and the radiator is ruptured, a handful of ground turmeric put in the radiator collects against the hole and patches it up long enough for you to get to the next town for repairs.

Chefs have been known to use turmeric to stop bleeding from cuts. A doctor at the Royal London Hospital was amazed when I applied it successfully to a cut in my arm. However, I don't recommend you try this at home!

Don't ask me why this is named Marie Kiteria. One day my chef, Mathias, suggested calling it this and the name has stuck. Marie Kiteria was his landlady in Goa and perhaps he had a secret affection for her – we shall never know.

You need to use mussels and clams on the half shell for this recipe. In Goa during the mango season, the half shells are left under a ripe mango tree. This attracts all the large red bully ants to the bottom of the tree so the pickers can scramble up and collect the fruit unhampered.

Shinanio Ani Tisreo Marie Kiteria

MUSSELS AND CLAMS IN COCONUT

Clean the mussels and clams and drain thoroughly. Toss in a bowl with the lime juice, turmeric and some salt, then set aside.

Heat 1 tablespoon of the oil in a large saucepan until hazy. Add the curry leaves, red chilies and cumin, then add the garlic and sauté for 1 minute. Add the onions and sauté until soft and pale. Stir in the coconut and cook for about 5 minutes, until it smells nutty and has turned pale golden.

Meanwhile, heat the remaining oil in a large heavy-bottomed frying pan until smoking. Drain the mussels and clams, adding their juices to the coconut and onion mixture. Put the seafood in the frying pan and sauté briskly for 3–4 minutes, stirring or tossing occasionally. Do not overcook.

Add the seafood to the coconut mixture. Mix well, stir in the cilantro and check the seasoning. Cook very briefly to blend the flavors, then serve immediately. It is best eaten with your fingers, although this can be a bit messy.

16 large mussels, on the half shell (preferably the New Zealand green-lipped variety)

32 large clams, on the half shell

juice of $1/2$ lime

$1/2$ tsp ground turmeric

2 tbsp oil

12 curry leaves

2 dried red chilies, snipped into small pieces

$1/2$ tsp cumin seeds

6–8 garlic cloves, very finely chopped

2 onions, finely chopped

9 oz fresh or thawed frozen grated coconut (see page 96)

2 tbsp chopped fresh cilantro

salt

This dish is very common in Goa, although recipes differ. Always select small squid, as the tubes are more delicate and tender. Serve with a salad and perhaps some baked potatoes.

Bhorlelay Mankyo

STUFFED SQUID

4 tbsp Balchao de Camarao (see page 121)

16 baby squid, about 3-5 in long, cleaned (tentacles retained and chopped)

5-7 oz small raw shrimp, chopped

3 hard-boiled eggs

1 tbsp chopped fresh cilantro

2 tbsp oil

salt

Drain as much oil out of the *balchao* as possible (you need about a tablespoon). Heat the *balchao* oil in a frying pan over high heat. Add the squid tentacles and the shrimp and sauté until just cooked. Drain off the oil by squeezing the mixture against the sides of the pan until it is dry. Stir the shrimp mixture into the *balchao*.

Separate the egg whites and yolks. Chop the whites finely and mash the yolks, then mix them both into the *balchao*. Stir in the cilantro, check the seasoning and divide the mixture into 16 portions. Spoon the mixture into the squid tubes, then pinch the ends together and run a small wooden toothpick through in a zigzag fashion. Snap off the ends of the toothpick, so there is only about $1/2$ in jutting out at either side.

Heat the oil in a large, heavy-bottomed frying pan, add the squid and cook over high heat for about 2 minutes on each side. If small, the squid will cook very fast. Do not overcook or they will become rubbery. Serve immediately.

Illustrated on previous pages

Crab is found in abundance all around the coast of India. Stuffed crab is not especially an Indian dish but in Goa. where the Portuguese influence has led to many Western cooking techniques being adopted, it becomes very Indian with a hint of Europe. You could use crab meat instead of whole crabs and serve it in ramekins or gratin dishes.

Crab à la Goa

Remove the crab meat from the shells and set aside. Wash and dry the shells. Heat the oil in a large, heavy-bottomed frying pan, add the ginger, garlic and green chilies and sauté for a minute or so. Add the onions and cook for 2–3 minutes, then add the *masala* and cook until the onions are soft and translucent. Add the ground coriander and turmeric and sauté, stirring, for 2–3 minutes. Stir in the tomatoes and cook for a few minutes longer, until the moisture has evaporated.

Now remove from the heat and season with salt. Mix in the crab meat, chopped cilantro and peas, then check the seasoning. You might need to add a few dashes of lemon juice.

Stuff the crab shells with the mixture and cover with the cheese. Place under a hot broiler to melt the cheese, then serve with a salad.

VARIATION
Add chopped hard-boiled egg and a few chopped shrimp.

SERVES 6

6 dressed crabs

2 tbsp sunflower or light olive oil

2-in piece of fresh ginger, finely chopped

5 garlic cloves, finely chopped

2 hot green chilies, finely chopped

2 onions, finely chopped

1½ tsp Piri-piri Masala (see page 123)

1½ tsp ground coriander

¼ tsp ground turmeric

2–3 tomatoes, chopped

1 tbsp chopped fresh cilantro

4 tbsp cooked peas

6 heaping tbsp grated medium-strong Cheddar cheese

lemon juice (optional)

salt

Lobster à l'Aguade

STUFFED LOBSTER

4 live lobsters, weighing
11-14 oz each

1 tsp lemon juice

½ tsp ground turmeric

1 oz butter

10 garlic cloves, finely chopped

2 hot green chilies, finely chopped

2 onions, finely chopped

1 tsp ground cumin

2 tsp ground coriander

4 slender green onions, chopped

2 tbsp chopped fresh cilantro

2 hard-boiled eggs, chopped
(optional)

2 tomatoes, seeded and diced
(optional)

salt

Place the live lobsters in the freezer for about 2 hours, then prepare as follows: with a large, sharp knife, pierce each lobster just below the base of the head, then with a firm sawing motion cut down through the tail to split the lobster in half, leaving the shell joined at the bottom. Next turn the lobster around and split the head in half in the same way, again leaving the shell joined underneath. Break off the claws and set aside. Remove the meat, greenish liver and coral, if any, from the lobster shells and set aside: discard the stomach sac from just behind the eyes and the black intestinal vein. Wash the shells, put them in a large pan of boiling water, along with the claws, and weight down to prevent them curling. Remove the claws after 2 minutes (this brief blanching makes the meat easier to extract) but boil the shells until they are a good red color. Rinse under cold running water, then drain well. The lobster shells are now your serving dishes.

Crack the claws and carefully remove the meat. Dice the raw lobster meat into ½-in pieces and toss with the lemon juice and turmeric, then stir in the claw meat.

Heat the butter in a large pan until foaming but not browned. Add the garlic and chilies and sauté for 2 minutes. Then add the onions and cook until soft. Stir in the cumin and coriander and sauté for a minute or two. Raise the heat to high and add the lobster meat and green onions. Mix the meat in briefly, then let it stay in the same position for a minute before you turn it around again. Do this only two or three times; the lobster will be cooked in 3–4 minutes, after which it will turn to rubber. Season with salt and remove from the heat. Remove the mixture from the pan with a slotted spoon and use to fill the shells. Place on serving plates and arrange the claws on the side as a garnish. Keep warm in a low oven.

Return the pan to the heat and boil to reduce the juices slightly. Add the cilantro and the chopped hard-boiled eggs and diced tomatoes, if using. Pour the sauce over the lobsters and serve immediately, with Pulao (see page 102) or plain steamed rice.

I created this extremely popular dish in Goa and named it after one of our chefs, who unfortunately for him always ended up making it. You will need very large tiger prawns weighing about 3-3½ oz each. These are available frozen in blocks from Asian and Chinese markets and are usually labeled '6-8' (which refers to the number per pound).

Tiger Prawns Aureliano

8 large, unshelled raw tiger prawns

lime juice

50 ml oil

1-2 large hot green chilies, finely chopped

5 garlic cloves, finely chopped

½ green bell pepper, finely diced

1 onion, finely chopped

½ tsp cumin seeds, crushed

½ tsp ground coriander

1 tomato, seeded and chopped

10-12 small shrimp (cooked or raw), shelled and chopped

a pinch of saffron strands

the white of 1 hard-boiled egg

1 tbsp chopped fresh cilantro

2-3 slices of bread, crusts removed, made into crumbs (or use a mixture of bread crumbs and grated Parmesan cheese)

butter for dotting

salt and pepper

With a small, sharp knife, slit the prawns from head to tail, cutting almost all the way through the flesh but being careful not to separate the halves. Remove the black intestinal vein running down the back of each prawn, then skewer the prawn on a bamboo skewer and open it out like a butterfly. Sprinkle with lime juice and some salt and pepper, then set aside for 30 minutes.

Heat the oil in a frying pan and sauté the green chilies and garlic until softened. Add the green bell pepper and onion and cook gently until the onion is translucent. Add the cumin and coriander, stir for a minute and then add the tomato. If using raw prawns, put them in now and sauté for 1-2 minutes, until cooked through. Stir in the saffron. Remove from the heat and stir in the chopped egg white, fresh cilantro and cooked tiger prawns, if using. Check the seasoning.

Stuff the mixture into the opened prawns. Sprinkle with the bread crumbs and dot with butter. Place the skewered prawns on a baking sheet and bake in an oven preheated to 375°F for 10-12 minutes. Do not overcook. Place near the top of the oven so that they color well. Alternatively, finish off under the broiler, taking care not to burn the crumbs.

Serve with finely shredded salad and ciabatta or garlic bread.

TIP
For best results, gently warm saffron strands in a dry frying pan for a few minutes, then soak them in a little water before use.

This is a Parsee specialty and the cooking of the potatoes is quite typical, though methods vary. For instance, if my mother were to make this she would cook the shrimp along with the potatoes. You can serve fried eggs on top of Masala Na Papeta, or bake beaten eggs on top of it.

Masala Na Papeta Ma Kolmi

SHRIMP WITH SPICY POTATOES

Wash the shrimp and drain thoroughly. Sprinkle them with the lime juice and some salt and set aside.

Purée the ingredients for the *masala* in a blender, adding a little more vinegar if necessary to make a smooth, thick paste. Mix with the potatoes and marinate for at least an hour to allow the spices to penetrate.

Heat the oil in a large pan over medium heat and sauté the curry leaves, garlic and green chilies for 2-3 minutes. Add the potatoes, along with all the *masala*. Sauté well for about 5 minutes, stirring frequently with a wooden spatula and scraping the bottom of the pan. Add just enough water to cover the potatoes, then cover the pan and simmer until the potatoes are almost done. Check whether the sauce around the potatoes is thick and rich looking. If it is too wet, simmer a little longer.

Increase the heat to high and add the shrimp. Level out the shrimp but do not stir or they will give off too much liquid and become rubbery. Cook on a high heat for 2-3 minutes, then season with salt to taste and sprinkle in the chopped cilantro.

If the sauce is still too thin, transfer some of the liquid to a separate pan and simmer until reduced and thickened, then return it to the pan (this is a useful technique when cooking shellfish, which should never be overcooked). Serve with hot *chapatis* or crusty bread.

1 lb shelled raw shrimp

2 tsp lime juice

1 lb potatoes, peeled and cut into $\frac{1}{2}$-in cubes

2 tbsp oil

5-8 curry leaves

8 very fresh green garlic cloves, with shoots, chopped (substitute 5 ordinary garlic cloves if necessary)

2 hot green chilies, finely chopped

3 tbsp chopped fresh cilantro

salt

For the masala:

8-10 dried red chilies, cut up and soaked in $1\frac{1}{2}$ tbsp malt vinegar until softened

1 tsp cumin seeds

4-5 garlic cloves

$\frac{1}{2}$ tsp ground turmeric

1 small onion, chopped

Meat, Poultry and Game

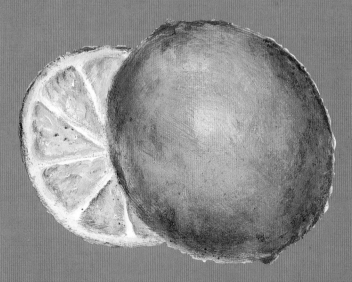

This dry meat dish makes an ideal accompaniment to curries and rice. It can also be served simply with plain rice and yogurt.

Ulathu

KERALAN DRY FRIED BEEF

Put all the ground spices in a dry frying pan and roast over low heat, stirring, for 1-2 minutes. Let cool, then rub into the beef, with some salt. Cover and refrigerate at least 3 hours, or overnight.

Heat half the *ghee* or oil in a frying pan, add the fresh coconut shavings and cook gently, stirring, until pale golden. Remove from the heat, drain on paper towels and set aside.

Heat the remaining oil or *ghee* in a separate pan and add any fat left from frying the coconut. Add the curry leaves and fry for 1 minute, then add the onion and garlic and fry until the onion is well browned. Remove from the pan with a slotted spoon and set aside. Add the beef and fry over high heat for about 5 minutes, tossing well so that it browns on all sides. When the liquid begins to evaporate, reduce the heat and cook for another 5-6 minutes. The meat should be about half done by now; if not, cover and cook for 5 minutes longer. Return the onion mixture to the pan and cook, uncovered, over low heat until the meat is almost done. Add the coconut and continue cooking until the meat is tender.

2 tsp ground dried red chili

3½ tsp ground coriander

1 tsp ground turmeric

1½ tsp ground cumin

1 lb sirloin steak, cut into ½-in cubes

2 tbsp ghee or 3 tbsp oil

flesh of ½ fresh coconut, cut into shavings on a mandoline or grater or with a vegetable peeler

12-15 curry leaves

1 large onion, finely sliced

6-8 garlic cloves, finely chopped

salt

VARIATION
If you omit the coconut and substitute 3 tablespoons of Ginger/Garlic Paste (see page 61) for the garlic, this recipe becomes Parsee in style.

A simple recipe for making delicious lamb patties, or cutlets as we call them. A very old recipe was discovered in Bombay recently. However, this version is named after my mother-in-law, who makes similar ones using sheep's brains.

Freny Aunty Na Lacy Cutless

1 onion, very finely chopped

oil for frying

1 lb fresh lean minced lamb (frozen meat will make the cutlets watery)

2-in piece of fresh ginger, very finely chopped

6-8 garlic cloves, very finely chopped

2 green chilies, very finely chopped

1 tsp ground cumin

$1^1/_2$ tsp ground coriander

$^1/_4$ tsp ground turmeric

$^1/_2$ tsp ground dried red chili

2 tbsp chopped fresh cilantro

2 tbsp chopped fresh mint

1 tsp lemon juice

3 slices of brown or white bread, soaked in a little water, then squeezed out into a ball

whole wheat flour

3-4 eggs

salt

MINCED LAMB CUTLETS

Fry the onion in 1 tablespoon of oil until soft. Remove from the heat and let cool. Mix with all the ingredients except the flour and eggs and knead well. To check the seasoning, fry a small ball of the mixture and taste. Adjust the seasoning if necessary.

Shape the lamb mixture into small balls and flatten them to about $^1/_4$ in thick. Smooth the edges so that the sides are not frayed, using either the base of your palm or a palette knife. Spread out some wholewheat flour out on a large flat plate or a baking dish and place each cutlet in it as you go along. Beat the eggs in a shallow bowl with some salt. Add 2 tablespoons of cold water and beat until the egg white is totally absorbed.

Pour some oil into a large frying pan to a depth of $^1/_4$ in and set on the heat. Coat the patties with flour, then dip in the beaten egg and fry in the hot oil for about 2 minutes per side. They should be a nice golden color with frilly edges. Drain on paper towels and keep warm in a low (275⁰F) oven while you fry the rest. Serve with Tamota Ni Gravy (see page 20).

Use the most tender lamb you can find.

Dhaniawala Gosht

LAMB WITH CORIANDER

Roast the coriander and cumin seeds in a dry frying pan, then remove from the heat and crush lightly in a mortar. Roast the dried chilies and cinnamon in a frying pan over low heat until they are aromatic and lightly colored. Cool and crush in a mortar or a small grinder to the consistency of crushed peppercorns.

Heat the oil in a saucepan until almost at smoking point and add the lamb. Cook over high heat until browned on all sides, then add the red chilies and cinnamon and sauté for a minute or two. Reduce the heat to medium, stir in the onions and cook, stirring constantly, until the base of the pan is scraped clean. Add a little water if necessary to help clean the pan. When the onions are translucent but not browned (they may go dark because of the pan juices, but this does not necessarily mean they are cooked), add the ginger, garlic and crushed cumin and coriander and sauté for a couple of minutes. Pour in water (or stock) just to cover the lamb. Season with salt, cover and simmer for 15–20 minutes. At this stage, if there is too much liquid, remove the lid and cook until the liquid has thickened and reduced. Stir in the tomatoes and cook on medium heat until the lamb is tender and the gravy is thick, not watery. Mix in the fresh cilantro and check the seasoning. Serve with plain steamed rice or bread.

2 tbsp coriander seeds

1 tbsp cumin seeds

4-5 dried red chilies, torn or snipped into pieces

2 x ¾-in pieces of cinnamon stick

4-5 tbsp oil

1 lb boned leg of lamb, cut into ¾-in cubes

3 onions, chopped

1 heaping tbsp very finely chopped fresh ginger

2 tbsp garlic, finely chopped

4 tomatoes, chopped, or 14-oz can of chopped tomatoes

3-4 tbsp chopped fresh cilantro

salt

Illustrated on next page

Dhansak

SERVES 6-8

For the wet masala:

2-in piece of cinnamon stick

6 cardamom pods

6-8 cloves

2 tsp cumin seeds

10 peppercorns

1 heaping tbsp coriander seeds

8-10 large dried red chilies

3 x ¾-in pieces of fresh ginger, coarsely chopped

10-12 garlic cloves, coarsely chopped

1-2 oz fresh cilantro (stalks and leaves)

For the dry masala:

3-4 cardamom pods

3-4 cloves

2-3 star anise

1 heaping tsp cumin seeds

8-10 peppercorns

2-3 dried red chilies

2 tsp dried fenugreek leaves

One of the greatest and best-known Parsee dishes, Dhansak has often been grossly abused by restaurants outside of India. This recipe is the real thing. *Dhan* means rice and *sak* refers to the legumes (*daal*) and lamb that go with it. To a Parsee, Dhansak is always made with lamb. It is not complete unless accompanied by *cachumber*, or onion salad, and deep-fried lamb kebabs.

Cooking Dhansak is a lengthy, painstaking affair but not difficult. The end result is a great achievement and, if done well, will be acclaimed as a masterpiece. Start it a day in advance to serve for lunch the following day.

This recipe comprises five separate stages – the *daal*, the lamb, the *pulao*, the kebabs and the salad – each of which can be served as an independent dish as well. This typifies the depth and intricacy of authentic Indian cooking.

You need to make two *masalas*: the wet one is for cooking with the lamb, while the dry one is added at the end as a flavoring. Both can be prepared in larger quantities and stored in airtight jars for up to 6 months. Keep the wet *masala* in the refrigerator and the dry one in your pantry. The dry *masala* is great for flavoring meat dishes at the last minute.

DAAL

Wash the lentils, peas and beans and place them in a large heavy-bottomed saucepan. Add enough water to cover by about $1/2$ in, then add all the remaining ingredients and bring to a boil. Reduce the heat and simmer, scraping the bottom of the pan frequently with a wooden spatula, until the legumes are tender. Purée everything until smooth, then cover and set aside.

LAMB

First prepare the *masalas*. For the wet *masala*, heat a large, heavy-bottomed frying pan or wok, add all the ingredients except the fresh cilantro and roast gently for about 5 minutes, stirring frequently. When the chilies and spices look roasted (i.e., they have changed color slightly but are not actually discolored) – remove and grind to a smooth paste in a blender, adding the fresh cilantro and just enough water to process the mixture.

For the dry *masala*, roast the spices as for the wet *masala*, then grind to a powder in a spice grinder.

Now cook the lamb. Heat the oil in a large heavy-bottomed saucepan, add the lamb and bones and sauté over high heat until the meat is well colored. Add the wet *masala* and cook until you see the oil separating out from it along the side of the pan. Add the water and some salt, cover tightly and cook over medium heat for 20-25 minutes, stirring occasionally and adding a little more water if the mixture looks too dry.

When the lamb is cooked and you have a nice thick, rich sauce, stir the mixture into the puréed *daal*. Add half the dry *masala*, then taste. If it is to your liking, save the rest of the *masala* to serve with other lamb dishes. Or add the rest of the *masala* a little at a time, tasting as you go.

This is your *sak*. We Parsees call this *masala ni daar ma gos*, meaning lamb in lentils cooked in *masala*. You can serve it on its own with any kind of rice if you do not want to make the *pulao* below. However, your Dhansak will be incomplete.

For the daal:

4 oz toover daal (yellow lentils)

2 oz channa daal (yellow split peas)

2 oz moong daal (mung beans)

4 oz masoor daal (pink lentils)

1 small eggplant, diced

4 oz pumpkin (peeled weight), diced

2 tbsp coarsely chopped fresh dill

1 colcasia leaf (arbi), if available

2 oz fresh fenugreek leaves, or 1 tbsp dried leaves, toasted (see page 9)

6 tbsp prepared tamarind pulp (see page 28) or paste or 2 tbsp concentrate

4 oz jaggery

2 tbsp chopped fresh cilantro stalks

2 tbsp chopped fresh mint stalks

salt

For the lamb:

2-3 tbsp oil

1 lb boned leg of lamb, cut into $3/4$-in cubes (ask your butcher to saw the bone up and give it to you)

5 fl oz water

chopped fresh cilantro and mint, to garnish

salt

To make the remaining Dhansak *dishes (the* Pulao, Kebabs *and* Cachumber *), see the next page*

Dhansak

continued from previous page

For the pulao:

5 tbsp oil

4 onions, finely sliced

1 tbsp chopped fresh mint

1 tbsp chopped fresh cilantro

¾-in piece of cinnamon stick

3-4 cardamom pods

3-4 cloves

4-5 star anise

1 lb basmati rice

about 2 tsp salt, to taste

For the cachumber:

1 large onion, finely sliced

10 fresh mint leaves, chopped

2 tsp chopped fresh cilantro

1 green chili, finely chopped

1 small tomato, seeded and finely chopped

1 tsp malt vinegar

salt

PULAO

Heat the oil in a large pan, add half the onions and fry until crisp and light golden (see page 103). Drain well on paper towels and set aside with the mint and cilantro (they will be used to garnish the rice just before serving). Add the spices to the pan and cook over fairly high heat for about 2 minutes, stirring, until dark and swollen. Add the remaining onions and cook gently, stirring frequently, until they are a deep brown color. Add the rice and cook over medium heat for 5-6 minutes, turning the rice regularly so that all the grains are evenly heated. Add the salt, then pour in enough hot water to cover the rice by about ¾ in. Stir for a minute, cover tightly and cook over very low heat for 15-20 minutes. Check the rice from time to time, stirring from the bottom up with a wooden spatula. If it seems to be drying out, add more water, just a little at a time. When the rice is done, set aside but do not uncover the pan.

KEBABS

Follow the recipe for Freny Aunty Na Lacy Cutless on page 54, making the mixture into balls about 1 inch in diameter. Omit the flour and egg coating. Deep-fry the kebabs or, if you prefer, place them on a greased baking sheet and bake in an oven preheated to 400°F for about 20 minutes. You can also cook them under a broiler if you rotate them regularly and check the cooking as you go along.

CACHUMBER

Mix all the ingredients together.

SERVING THE DHANSAK

Reheat the rice, lamb and kebabs if necessary. Garnish the *pulao* with the fried onions, mint and fresh cilantro, then dot the kebabs over the top. Garnish the *sak* with chopped fresh cilantro and mint. Serve with the *cachumber*, and with fried *papads* (*papadums*) if you like. These should be lentil *papads*, not the Madras ones.

This is a typical simple Parsee lamb dish. It is one of my favorites, particularly when served with Dhan Daar Nay Vaghaar (see page 103).

Kharu Gos

LAMB WITH WHOLE SPICES AND ONIONS

Heat the oil in a heavy saucepan until a haze forms on top. Add the cinnamon, cardamom, cloves and red chilies. As soon as the spices swell and change color, add the onions and sauté until well browned. Add the lamb and cook, turning occasionally, until browned on all sides. When the liquid in the pan has almost dried up, add the ground spices and the ginger/garlic paste and stir well. Then add some salt and enough water (or stock) to just about cover the lamb. Cover with a tight-fitting lid and simmer for 15-20 minutes, stirring from time to time and making sure the sides of the pan are kept clean.

Add the potatoes and mix them in well, then add the tomato, if using. Cover again and simmer until the lamb and potatoes are tender. Check the seasoning and sprinkle with some chopped fresh cilantro. Stir some in as well, if you like, for an extra kick.

GINGER/GARLIC PASTE
Ginger/garlic paste forms the basis of most of India's cooking. In many recipes in this book I have listed finely chopped garlic and ginger separately to make life easier. However, in some recipes only a paste will do. Most supermarkets now sell separate jars of ginger paste and garlic paste. All you need to do is blend them together.

To make your own, take equal quantities of peeled garlic and fresh ginger and work them to a paste with a mortar and pestle. Alternatively, purée them in a blender with a little water and some bland vegetable oil (not olive oil), stopping regularly to scrape down the sides. The paste will keep in the refrigerator for up to 2 months if you mix in a little oil to prevent spoiling.

2-3 tbsp oil

¾-in piece of cinnamon stick

3-4 green cardamom pods

1-2 black cardamom pods, if available

2-3 cloves

2-3 dried red chilies, torn or snipped into pieces

2 onions, chopped

1 lb boned leg of lamb, cut into ¾-in cubes (ask your butcher to saw up the bone and give it to you)

1 tbsp ground cumin

1½ tbsp ground coriander

½ tsp ground turmeric

1 heaping tbsp Ginger/Garlic Paste (see left)

1-2 large potatoes, peeled and cut into large chunks

1 tomato, chopped (optional)

chopped fresh cilantro, for garnish

salt

This spicy lamb dish is cooked with whole *garam masala*, fried red chilies, onions and yogurt. It is similar to a classic *rogan josh* but hotter. If you have time, marinate the lamb with the ginger/garlic paste overnight.

Khadey Masaley Ka Gosht

SERVES 6

4-5 onions, finely sliced

7 oz oil or ghee

8-10 large dried red chilies, broken or snipped into pieces

2-3 green chilies, slit lengthwise

2 x 1½-in pieces of cinnamon stick

5-6 cardamom pods

4-5 cloves

4-5 peppercorns

1-2 blades of mace

1 lb boned leg of lamb, cut into ¾-in cubes (ask your butcher to saw the bone up and give it to you)

2 tbsp Ginger/Garlic Paste (see page 61)

4-5 tomatoes, chopped, or 9 oz canned tomatoes

7 oz Greek-style yogurt

1-2 tbsp chopped fresh cilantro

salt

To garnish:

1 large potato, boiled, cut into cubes and fried until brown

2-3 eggs, hard-boiled and cut into wedges

LAMB WITH WHOLE SPICES, CHILIES AND YOGURT

Fry the onions in the oil or *ghee* until golden and crisp (see page 103) and then set aside. Fry the red and green chilies in the same oil for 2 minutes over medium heat, until they are just getting darker, then set aside with the onions.

Reheat the oil or *ghee* in a large heavy-bottomed saucepan until it forms a haze, then add the whole spices. Sauté for a minute or so until they swell and change color. Add the lamb (and bone) and increase the heat to maximum. Stir once to level out the lamb, then cook, stirring as little as possible, until the lamb is well browned on all sides. (If you find the bottom of the pan is browning too rapidly, add a couple of tablespoons of water, scrape with a wooden spoon and continue cooking.)

Reduce the heat to medium. Add the ginger/garlic paste and sauté for 5-6 minutes. Cover the pan and cook for 20 minutes, stirring from time to time to prevent sticking. Do not worry, though, if the bottom of the pan is covered with a brown film. Add the tomatoes and some salt and continue cooking until the tomatoes have broken down.

Purée the fried onions and chilies with the yogurt and add to the lamb. Cook uncovered for 5-10 minutes, then cover and simmer until the lamb is tender. Check the seasoning and stir in the cilantro. If there is too much oil on top, skim it off and save for another lamb dish.

Remove from the heat and serve garnished with the fried potato and hard-boiled eggs. *Chapatis* or *parathas* make the best accompaniment.

This dish is regarded as a delicacy in some parts of Pakistan, where the best fenugreek (*methi*) grows. If you use fresh fenugreek for this recipe it will probably be the large variety. The small-leafed fenugreek is hard to find but if you do have it, halve the quantity given below to 2 oz and soak it in salted water for 30 minutes to soften the bitter flavor.

Methi Murgh

CHICKEN WITH FENUGREEK

1 lb boneless chicken breasts

7 oz Greek-style yogurt

1 tsp lemon juice (optional)

2 fl oz ghee or oil

5-6 long green chilies, finely chopped (and seeded, if you like)

8 garlic cloves, finely chopped

2-in piece of fresh ginger, half finely chopped, half cut into thin strips

11 oz onions, finely chopped

1 tsp ground coriander

1 tsp ground dried red chili

7 oz tomatoes, chopped

7 fl oz water

2 tbsp dried fenugreek (Qasuri methi), toasted (see page 9) or 4½ oz fresh fenugreek leaves, chopped

2 tbsp chopped fresh cilantro

salt

For the whole masala:

5-6 green cardamom pods

1 black cardamom pod, if available

5-6 cloves

¾-in piece of cinnamon stick (in India and Pakistan acacia bark is used)

1 bay leaf

1 blade of mace

1 tsp cumin seeds

In India or at home, we would only cook chicken on the bone, but boneless breast makes the dish more special and easier to eat. Cut the chicken into whatever size pieces you prefer and remove the skin if you like. Beat the yogurt with the lemon juice, if using, and some salt and mix in the chicken. Set aside for about an hour.

Heat the *ghee* or oil in a large pan until a haze appears on top. Reduce the heat and add the ingredients for the whole *masala* (putting the cumin seeds in last as they are more likely to burn). Cook until the spices are swollen and colored, then stir in the green chilies, garlic and finely chopped ginger. When the garlic begins to turn golden, add the onions and the ground coriander and ground chili mixed with about 4 tablespoons of water – this prevents the ground spices burning and also allows the color to come through better. Cook until the onions are soft. Now stir in the tomatoes and cook gently until the fat begins to surface. Add the chicken and its marinade, then the water. Stir well and simmer, covered, stirring occasionally, for about 10 minutes, until the chicken is almost cooked. Stir in the fenugreek, cilantro and the strips of ginger and cook for a few minutes more, until the chicken is done. Check the seasoning and remove from the heat. If you are using fresh fenugreek you will need to cook it a little longer.

Serve with soft corn tortillas, which are similar to Indian corn *chapatis*, or with warm Indian breads.

A delicate and mild dish that will please even the most chili-fearing and unadventurous.

Malai Murg Tikka

CREAMY CHICKEN TIKKA

3 skinless boneless chicken breasts, cut into quarters

1 tsp lemon juice

1 tbsp heavy cream

3 tbsp Greek-style yogurt

1½ tbsp finely grated Cheddar cheese

1 tbsp Ginger/Garlic Paste (see page 61)

6 cardamom pods, ground, or 1 tsp ground cardamom

½ tsp ground cumin

½ tsp ground nutmeg

1 small hot green chili, finely chopped (optional, but it gives a good flavor)

1 tbsp mustard oil

melted butter for basting

salt

Sprinkle the chicken with the lemon juice and some salt, place in a bowl and set aside.

In another bowl, whisk all the remaining ingredients except the melted butter together until the cheese blends in. Mix in the chicken, check the seasoning, then cover and refrigerate for at least 3 hours, preferably overnight.

Like all other *tikkas*, this is best grilled over charcoal. If you wish to cook it under a broiler, place all the chicken pieces on a baking sheet, touching each other, baste with a little melted butter and broil under medium-high heat until golden brown. Turn the chicken over carefully so that the pieces do not separate and broil until the other side is browned. The total cooking time should be about 12-15 minutes.

If grilling, don't place the chicken directly on the grill or it will stick. Instead, skewer the pieces and support the skewers so they are just above the grill. Cook, turning, until the chicken is browned all over.

This very popular Parsee dish is served on festive occasions such as weddings. The Parsee tradition of cooking with fruit, both fresh and dried, dates back to our Persian ancestry. Try to find Indian or Pakistani dried apricots, available from most Indian markets. They have a richer, less tart flavor than the ordinary variety. Pit them if you prefer, but we like to leave the pits in, then crack them later and eat the kernels.

This is very good served with crispy straw potatoes, or *sali*. *Chapatis*, bread or plain rice also make suitable accompaniments.

Jardaloo Ma Murghi

CHICKEN WITH APRICOTS

Soak the apricots overnight in about 8 fl oz cold water (or soak them for 2-3 hours in warm water), until swollen and soft.

Grind together all the ingredients for the *masala* and set aside.

Heat the oil in a large heavy-bottomed pan and add the cinnamon sticks. After 1-2 minutes, when they are slightly swollen, add the onions and brown slowly. Then stir in the *masala* and sauté until the oil begins to separate from it. Add the chicken and sauté for about 5 minutes. Season, then add the tomatoes and apricots, plus any of the soaking water that has not been absorbed. Mix well, cover and simmer until the chicken is tender. If the sauce is too thin, uncover and cook for a few minutes longer until it has reduced and thickened. Stir in the chopped cilantro and check the seasoning.

7 oz dried apricots

4 tbsp oil

2 x ¾-in pieces of cinnamon stick

2 onions, chopped

1-1¼-in boned chicken, cut into ¾-in dice

4 tomatoes, chopped

1-2 tbsp chopped fresh cilantro

salt

For the masala:

6-8 large dried red chilies

1½ tsp cumin seeds

1½ tbsp coriander seeds

¾-in piece of cinnamon stick

4-5 green cardamom pods

4-5 cloves

2 heaping tbsp Ginger/Garlic Paste (see page 61)

This is my version of a Goan recipe with obvious Western roots. I love it and it has created waves on my menus in both England and Goa. Serve with garlic rice, made by sautéing some garlic and chopped green onions in a little oil until softened, then stirring in cooked rice and heating it through.

Galinha Cafreal

8 chicken thighs

3 fl oz oil

2 medium onions, finely chopped

¾-in piece of fresh ginger, shredded

1 large hot green chili, shredded

¼ tsp ground turmeric

½ tsp ground cumin

½ tsp ground coriander

8 fl oz coconut milk (canned is fine)

For the masala:

5-6 large green chilies

5-6 black peppercorns

2-in piece of fresh ginger

8-10 garlic cloves

4-5 large deep-red dried chilies

4 tbsp chopped fresh cilantro

2 tbsp lemon juice

1 tsp cumin seeds

2 tsp coriander seeds

salt

For the garnish:

oil for frying

1 large onion, cut into thick rings

1 large potato, peeled and finely sliced

1-2 tomatoes, sliced

CHICKEN GOAN-STYLE

First make the *masala*: grind all the ingredients except the salt to a thick paste in a blender or a mortar and pestle, adding a little water if you use a blender. Add salt to taste. Pierce the chicken thighs with a fork and rub the *masala* liberally into them. Cover and leave for at least 3 hours, preferably overnight in the refrigerator.

Heat the oil in a heavy-bottomed frying pan set over medium heat. Place the chicken in it skin-side down and allow to brown slowly, shaking the pan gently so that the skin does not stick. When golden, turn over and continue to cook until the chicken is done (test with a skewer; the juices should run clear). Transfer to a dish and keep warm in a low (275°F) oven.

Put the pan back on the heat and add the onions, ginger, green chili, turmeric, cumin and coriander. Sauté until the onions are browned, then stir in the coconut milk and simmer for 10-12 minutes, until the sauce has thickened to a pouring consistency.

Next prepare the garnish. In another pan, heat just enough oil to coat the base and then sauté the onion rings until brown. Remove from the pan and set aside. Add the potato slices to the pan and sauté until brown and tender.

Serve the chicken with the garnish. The sauce can either be served separately or poured over the chicken.

The term *vindaloo* comes from the Portuguese *vindalho*, meaning with vinegar and garlic. The Goans, of course, could not stop at this. With their spicy palate, they invented the *vindaloo* as we know it today. In England, *vindaloo* is much misunderstood, and is thought to mean a fiery hot curry. In fact a *vindaloo* is a hot, sweet and sour curry made with the notorious Goan red *masala*, and the degree of heat can vary from house to house, chef to chef. In Goa and Mangalore a *vindaloo* is always made with pork. However, it works well with several other meats.

This recipe is for a basic chicken *vindaloo*. You could substitute leg of pork, cut into ¾-in cubes, in which case reduce the quantity of oil by half and sauté the pork before adding the onions.

Vindaloo de Frango

CHICKEN VINDALOO

Heat the oil in a large saucepan, add the curry leaves and sauté for a few seconds. Add the onions and sauté until a deep golden brown. Stir in the *masala* and cook until the oil separates out from it. Add the chicken and cook until well browned. Stir in the stock or water, then add the tamarind and sugar, bring to a boil and simmer for about 15 minutes or until the chicken is cooked through. Season with salt and then serve with Pulao (see page 102) or crusty bread.

Peeled baby potatoes and cocktail onions or shallots may be added along with the chicken, or halfway through the cooking time if you are using pork.

4 tbsp oil

a few curry leaves

3 onions, finely chopped

5-7 oz Piri-piri Masala
(see page 123)

1¾-2 lb chicken thighs

8 fl oz chicken stock or water

1 tbsp prepared tamarind pulp
(see page 28) or paste, or
1 tsp concentrate

1 tsp sugar

salt

Murghi Na Farcha

CURRIED CHICKEN FRIED IN EGG

2 tbsp oil

2-in piece of cinnamon stick

4-5 green cardamom pods

3-4 cloves

1-2 hot green chilies, slit lengthwise

8 chicken thighs

1 onion, finely sliced

2 tbsp Ginger/Garlic Paste (see page 61)

1 tbsp ground dried red chili

1 tsp ground cumin

2 tsp ground coriander

½ tsp ground turmeric

2 tomatoes, chopped

2 tbsp chopped fresh cilantro

1 tbsp chopped fresh mint

oil for frying

3 eggs, beaten with 1 tbsp water

4-5 tbsp all-purpose flour

salt

Heat the oil in a large frying pan over medium heat. Add the cinnamon, cardamom, cloves and chilies and sauté for a minute, then push to one side of the pan. Add the chicken skin-side down, and cook until well browned, then brown the other side. Remove the chicken from the pan and set aside. Add the onion to the pan and sauté for 2 minutes, then stir in the ginger/garlic paste, ground spices, tomatoes and half the chopped cilantro. Cook for a few minutes until you have a thick, dry mixture, then return the chicken to the pan (you could also add a couple of tablespoons of tomato ketchup; I must admit I do). Mix well, then cover and simmer for about 10 minutes, until the chicken is cooked through. Mix in the remaining cilantro and the mint and let cool, covered.

Transfer the chicken to a plate, scraping off excess sauce, such as onion pieces. Do not wipe the chicken clean, however; it should have a light coating of sauce but should not be wet.

Pour some oil into a large frying pan to a depth of about ¼ in and heat until you see a slight haze. Coat the chicken pieces in the flour, then dip them in the egg, making sure they are completely coated. Lift them out of the egg, draining off excess, and then fry in the oil until golden brown. The egg must frizzle, giving a lacy texture. Do not discard the bits that float on the oil. When you serve the chicken you can sprinkle the bits of fried egg on top.

Drain the chicken on paper towels. Purée the sauce if you like, then reheat it. Dilute as necessary and serve with the chicken.

VARIATIONS
• Flavor the beaten eggs with spices, such as ground dried red chilies, salt and a touch of turmeric.

• You could add tiny new potatoes, cooking them in the sauce. We Parsees love potatoes and no meal is complete without them.

Badak Chaanti Badami Pasanda

NUT-STUFFED DUCK BREAST

Mix together all the ingredients for the stuffing, then taste and adjust the seasoning if necessary. Chill until firm.

Trim some of the skin and fat from the duck breasts but do not remove it all. Slit the breasts horizontally through the center, leaving them joined at one side. If you do this gently, using short strokes, the meat will separate fairly cleanly. Open out the breasts and lay them in a row. If necessary, beat them out a little to make them easier to roll up. Spoon the stuffing along the top edge of each breast (the wider end), then fold the edge over the stuffing and roll up into a sausage shape. Roll each breast in a piece of foil or wax paper and place in a saucepan large enough to hold them all in a single layer. Pour in enough boiling water to come a little above the rolls, then cover and simmer for 20 minutes. Let cool in the liquid, then skim off any fat. Reserve the liquid.

To make the sauce, heat the butter in a large pan until foaming. When the foam subsides slightly, add the onions and sauté for 5-6 minutes, until translucent. Stir in the ginger/garlic paste and all the ground spices and sauté for 2-3 minutes. Next add the ground almonds and the cashew nuts and sauté for 4-5 minutes, stirring. Stir in 8 fl oz of the duck cooking liquid and simmer for 15 minutes, until fairly thick. If it gets too thick, add more cooking liquid or water. Let cool and purée in a blender. Return to the heat and bring slowly to a boil, stirring frequently.

Meanwhile, heat the *ghee* for the tempering in a separate pan and fry the whole spices and the bay leaves until dark and swollen. Add them to the sauce and stir well. Check the seasoning.

To serve, remove the foil or greaseproof paper from the duck breasts and place them in the sauce. Warm very gently so that the duck heats through. Place the breasts on a platter and pour the sauce over. Garnish with slivers of almond and pistachios.

SERVES 6

6 duck breasts

slivers of almonds and pistachio nuts, for garnish

For the stuffing:

5 oz ricotta or finely grated paneer

6-8 unskinned almonds, coarsely chopped

6-8 pistachio nuts, coarsely chopped

1 heaping tbsp golden raisins

a generous pinch or two of ground cardamom

1 tbsp chopped fresh cilantro

a small pinch of saffron strands

salt

For the sauce:

1 oz butter

2 onions, sliced

1 tbsp Ginger/Garlic Paste (see page 61)

¼ tsp ground turmeric

½ tsp ground cumin

¾ tsp ground coriander

½ tsp ground dried red chili

4 oz ground almonds

4 oz cashew nuts

For the tempering:

1 tbsp ghee (or half butter/half oil)

¾-in piece of cinnamon stick

3-4 cardamom pods

3 cloves

2 peppercorns

1 blade of mace, broken in half

1-2 bay leaves

Toofan Mail was India's best-known mail train, thundering from Dehradun in the north to Bombay on the southwest coast, and boasting a very good dining car. Its name came to be used for any fast-moving vehicle or a product that sold fast.

I invented this *tikka* a few years ago and made it primarily with venison until ostrich, which has similar properties to venison, became available. Whether you use venison or ostrich, this recipe should not disappoint.

Venison Tikka Toofan Mail

1 tsp salt

1 lb venison or ostrich (either fillet or leg), cut into ¾-in cubes, or into thin slices if barbecuing

2 tbsp sesame oil or mustard oil

¾-in piece of cinnamon stick

3-4 green cardamom pods

2-3 star anise

1 tsp fennel seeds

8-10 garlic cloves, coarsely chopped

¾-in piece of fresh ginger, coarsely chopped

2-3 hot green chilies, coarsely chopped

3-4 large dried red chilies, torn or snipped into pieces

stalks from 1 bunch of cilantro (save the leaves for garnishes, chutneys etc.)

9 oz Greek-style yogurt

1 tbsp lemon juice

Rub the salt into the meat and set aside.

Meanwhile, heat the oil in a pan, add all the remaining ingredients except the yogurt and lemon juice and cook gently, taking care not to let them color. Stir frequently until the heat has penetrated right through and the dried chilies are gently roasting. Let cool and then grind to a smooth paste in a blender with the yogurt and lemon juice, making sure all the spices are fully ground.

Rub the paste into the meat and check the salt. Place in a clean bowl, cover and leave at room temperature for about 2 hours, then transfer to the refrigerator for 8-10 hours. (For a dense meat such as ostrich, an overnight marinade is essential.)

To cook the meat, broil under high heat or grill on a barbecue, turning after about 3-4 minutes. Once it is well colored on both sides, check a piece for tenderness. Be careful not to overcook it. Serve with a salad and Pulao (see page 102), to which you have added green peas..

This is a Rajasthani-style preparation, generally made with wild boar, although hare, venison, buffalo and game birds such as pheasant and partridge are also very good. This recipe is a simple version that will work with most meats. It is a pungent dish but, believe me, you will relish every morsel. It keeps very well in the refrigerator.

Jungli Laal Maas

HOT RAJASTHANI GAME

1 lb game meat, cleaned and cut into cubes (or cut into pieces on the bone if using birds)

¹/₂ tsp ground turmeric

3-4 onions, finely sliced

3-4 tbsp ghee

2 tbsp oil

2-in piece of cinnamon stick

3-4 green cardamom pods

3-4 cloves

2 blades of mace

1 large dried red chili, broken in half

11 oz Greek-style yogurt

2 tomatoes, chopped

chopped fresh cilantro, to serve

salt

For the masala:

2-in piece of fresh ginger, roughly chopped

10-12 garlic cloves

6-8 long dark-red dried chilies

1 heaping tsp cumin seeds

1 tbsp coriander seeds

Rub the meat with the turmeric and some salt and set aside.

Next make the *masala*: put all the ingredients in a blender with a little water and blend to a thick paste.

Fry the onions in the *ghee* until golden brown and crisp (see page 103), then set aside.

Heat the oil in a large heavy-bottomed saucepan and add any *ghee* left over from frying the onions. Add the cinnamon, cardamom pods, cloves, mace and red chili and sauté over medium heat for 2 minutes, until the spices change color and swell. Do not let the chili burn, but don't worry if it gets a bit dark.

Now add the meat and fry until evenly browned. Do not stir it too much or the oil will cool down and the meat will give off its juices. Add the *masala* and sauté for 4-5 minutes, until the oil begins to separate out from it. Add enough water to come about ¹/₄ in above the meat, then cover the pan and simmer until the meat is about three-quarters done.

Purée the fried onions with the yogurt and stir into the meat. Add the tomatoes and stir well, scraping the sides of the pan. Cover and continue to cook until the meat is tender. Check the seasoning and sprinkle with chopped fresh cilantro. Serve with hot *chapatis* or flour tortillas.

These dry kebabs can be made with other game, such as bison or even ostrich. The recipe is quite time-consuming but you can simplify it by omitting the skewering and frying at the end.

Jungli Soover Ni Seek Boti

VENISON KEBABS

Put the meat in a bowl with the ginger/garlic paste, ground spices and lemon juice and mix until coated. Cover and set aside for 2-3 hours to allow the spices to penetrate, then transfer to the refrigerator for 5-6 hours, preferably overnight.

Heat 2 tablespoons of oil almost to smoking point in a heavy-bottomed saucepan. Add the meat (reserving any liquid) and stir for a few minutes until well browned; don't be alarmed by the residue at the bottom of the pan. Add 1-2 tablespoons of water and the marinade juices, scrape the bottom of the pan with a wooden spatula, check the salt, then cover tightly and cook over fairly low heat. After about 20 minutes, remove the lid and cook until the liquid has just about dried out and the meat has a thick coating on it and is almost cooked through. Remove from the heat and stir in the green chili, cilantro, ginger and garlic. Let cool, then mix once again. Next skewer the meat on small bamboo skewers, putting about 4 pieces on each. You can snap off one end if they are too long.

Spread the flour out on a large flat plate. Beat the eggs with a pinch or two of salt in a dish large enough to hold the kebabs. Pour enough oil into a large frying pan to fill it to a depth of about $^{1}/_{4}$ in and set it over medium heat. If the oil gets too hot the egg will brown instantly and the kebabs will not heat right through. (If this does happen, place the kebabs on paper towels in a moderate (350°F) oven for a few minutes before serving.)

Roll the kebabs in the flour, dip them in the beaten egg and fry for 1-2 minutes per side. Don't worry if there is extra egg on the skewers; this will help make the kebabs frilly.

Serve with chutney, such as the Green Chutney on page 25 or a hot, ketchup-type sauce.

1 lb venison, cut into $^{3}/_{4}$-in cubes

2 tbsp Ginger/Garlic Paste
(see page 61)

$^{1}/_{2}$ tsp ground turmeric

2 tsp ground coriander

1 tsp ground cumin

1 tsp ground dried red chili

$^{1}/_{2}$ tsp garam masala
(see page 123)

1 tbsp lemon juice

oil for frying

1 large hot green chili, finely chopped

1 tbsp chopped fresh cilantro

$^{1}/_{4}$-in piece of fresh ginger, very finely chopped

2 garlic cloves, very finely chopped

3-4 tbsp all-purpose flour

2 eggs

salt

Illustrated on next page

This recipe dates back centuries. You can use whatever combination of game you like. depending on what is available. The koftas are served in a rich sauce but you could also serve them with Green Coconut Chutney (see page 36) or a raita (see page 118).

Shikari Nargisi Kofta

7 oz venison

7 oz hare

7 oz wild boar

2-in piece of fresh ginger

8 garlic cloves

2 hot green chilies

3-4 fresh cilantro sprigs

8-10 fresh mint leaves

1½ tsp salt

1 tsp garam masala (see page 123)

4 eggs

For the sauce:

2 tbsp oil

3 onions, very finely chopped

2-in piece of fresh ginger, chopped

8 garlic cloves

3-4 large dried red chilies

1 tsp cumin seeds

1 tbsp coriander seeds

½ tsp fennel seeds

2-in piece of cinnamon stick, broken up

½ tsp ground turmeric

10-12 cashew nuts

1 heaping tbsp ground almonds

8-9 oz Greek-style yogurt

salt

INDIAN GAME SCOTCH EGG

Finely chop together the meat. ginger. garlic. chilies. cilantro. mint. salt and *garam masala*. preferably twice to get a fine texture. Check the seasoning (fry a small piece and taste it). then set the mixture aside.

Hard-boil the eggs for 7-8 minutes, then drain. Cool gently under slow running water. shell the eggs and cut them in half.

Divide the chopped meat mixture into 8 portions and work each piece with your hands until soft and supple. Flatten each portion in your palm and place an egg half in the center. Pull the mixture around the egg to enclose it completely and then shape it into a *kofta*, or ball. You can make it egg-shaped if you like or keep it round. The *koftas* are now cooked in the sauce. but if you prefer you can deep-fry them or bake them in a moderate (350°F) oven.

To make the sauce. heat the oil in a pan over medium heat. add the onions and sauté until a rich. dark brown, stirring frequently. Meanwhile put all the remaining ingredients in a blender and purée until smooth. When the onions are browned. add the puréed mixture and stir continuously for 2-3 minutes, until it begins to bubble. Reduce the heat. cover and cook for 15 minutes. stirring and scraping the bottom of the pan from time to time. If it becomes too thick. add some water or stock.

Check the seasoning and cook for a further 10-12 minutes. until a thin film of oil comes to the surface. Add the raw *koftas* and cook covered for 20 minutes on a slow simmer. If you are adding them cooked you only have to simmer them for a few minutes until heated.

Crocodile has firm, lean flesh that tastes rather like pork. It is eaten in the heart of India, where crocodiles are found, by the Bhil tribes. This recipe is my invention, however, combining a traditional sauce with an unusual meat. *Ambotik* means sour and hot, and is a Goan curry, normally prepared with fish such as shark, skate or sting ray. Some supermarkets now sell crocodile meat or you can buy it from specialty butchers.

Crocodile Ambotik

Rub the lemon juice and some salt into the crocodile fillet and set aside.

Grind together all the ingredients for the *masala*, adding enough vinegar to make a smooth, thick paste.

Heat 3 tablespoons of the oil in a pan, add the onion and fry until golden brown. Add the *masala* and fry for 8-10 minutes or until the oil begins to separate out from it. Add the chopped tomatoes and cook for 4-5 minutes, until they have broken down. Stir in the water and simmer for 8-10 minutes.

Heat the remaining oil in a heavy-bottomed frying pan and sauté the crocodile slices on high until golden brown on each side. Add them to the sauce and simmer for just a few minutes, until tender. Do not overcook as the crocodile meat can become tough. Check the seasoning and serve with steamed rice.

$1^{1}/_{2}$ **tbsp lemon juice**

1 lb crocodile tail fillet, cut into slices about $^{1}/_{4}$-$^{1}/_{2}$ in thick

5 tbsp oil

1 onion, finely sliced

3 tomatoes, chopped

7 fl oz water

salt

For the masala:

10 dried red Kashmiri chilies

$^{1}/_{2}$ **tsp cumin seeds**

$^{1}/_{2}$ **tsp ground turmeric**

6-8 peppercorns

3 cloves

3 cardamom pods

$^{1}/_{4}$-**in piece of cinnamon stick**

4-5 garlic cloves

$^{1}/_{4}$-**in piece of fresh ginger**

2 tbsp prepared tamarind pulp (see page 28) or paste, or 2 tsp concentrate

palm vinegar (substitute cider vinegar if not available)

Vegetable Dishes and Accompaniments

Do piaza is a Mughal term which, strictly speaking, means something that is added to or cooked with a meat dish. For instance, lamb cooked with okra is *gosht do piaza bhindi*. However, hotels and restaurants in India have corrupted the term so that it now refers to a dish cooked with onion cubes, or with double the quantity of onions.

Paneer Do Piaza

PANEER WITH ONION, GREEN PEPPER AND TOMATO

Heat the oil in a large pan, add the cumin seeds and cook for a minute or two, then add the onion, garlic and ginger and sauté until softened. Stir in the ground chili, ground coriander and turmeric and cook for 1-2 minutes. Stir in the green bell pepper and tomato and cook until the pepper is softened. Now add the *paneer* and sauté for another 4-5 minutes. Stir in the chopped cilantro, salt to taste and the *garam masala* if using. Garnish with tomato wedges and serve.

VARIATION
Okra, diced chicken, shrimp and fish can all be substituted for the paneer.

TO PREPARE PANEER
Paneer is a whey cheese that is now available in Indian markets and some large supermarkets but is also easy to make at home.
For a 7 oz paneer, bring 70 fl oz whole milk to a boil, then stir in 8 tablespoons of live yogurt and simmer until it curdles. Strain through a sieve lined with a large piece of cheesecloth. Once drained, transfer to a tray, fold the ends of the cheesecloth over the solids and put a weight on top. Let sit until all the moisture has been squeezed out. Store the pressed cheese in the refrigerator.

Before paneer is added to a dish, it must be cut into cubes and deep-fried in oil until golden, then drained and put in a bowl of water. Squeeze out well before use. Once fried, it can be stored in its bowl of water in the refrigerator for 6 days.

3 tbsp oil

1 heaping tsp cumin seeds

1 onion, cut into 8 pieces

6-8 garlic cloves, finely chopped

¾-in piece of fresh ginger, shredded

1 tsp ground dried red chili

2 tsp ground coriander

a pinch of ground turmeric

1 green bell pepper, cut into 8 pieces

1 large tomato, cut into 8 pieces

9 oz paneer, cut into cubes, deep-fried and soaked (see left)

2 tbsp chopped fresh cilantro

1 tsp garam masala (see page 123) (optional)

tomato wedges, to garnish

salt

Bhurjee means minced or finely chopped and generally refers to foods such as eggs, *paneer* and chicken. This simple recipe makes a great quick meal. It goes best with a pea *pulao* or *chapatis* and a sweetish chutney.

Paneer Bhurjee

SPICY MINCED PANEER

2 tbsp oil

6 garlic cloves, finely chopped

1 tbsp finely chopped fresh ginger

1-2 hot green chilies, chopped

1 heaping tsp crushed cumin seeds

2 small to medium onions, chopped

$\frac{1}{4}$ tsp ground turmeric

$\frac{1}{2}$ tsp ground dried red chili

2 tomatoes, seeded and chopped

14 oz paneer, mashed with a fork

$1\frac{1}{2}$ tbsp chopped fresh cilantro

$\frac{1}{2}$ tsp chaat masala

salt

Heat the oil in a saucepan, add the garlic, ginger and green chili and sauté over medium heat until the garlic begins to color. Add the cumin and sauté for a minute or two, then add the onions. Cook until the onions are soft, then stir in the turmeric and ground dried red chili. Increase the heat to high and add the tomatoes. Sauté for 2-3 minutes, until the tomato juices begin to dry up, being careful the mixture does not stick. Lower the heat to medium once again and gently stir in the *paneer*. Cook until well heated through. Add salt to taste, then stir in the fresh cilantro. Remove from the heat, sprinkle with the *chaat masala* and serve.

These croquettes are stuffed with nuts and cheese and simmered in a spicy spinach sauce. You can also make smaller ones and serve them as a delightful snack with any cream-based dip you like.

Malai Kofta Palakwala

POTATO AND CHEESE CROQUETTES WITH SPINACH SAUCE

Boil and mash the potatoes, drying them out well (see page 24). Season with salt and pepper.

For the stuffing, grate the cheese, then mix with all the remaining ingredients and check the seasoning. Shape the mashed potato into balls the size of an egg, then stuff each one with about 2 tablespoons of the filling. The easiest way to do this is to flatten the ball in your palm, add the stuffing, then pull the mashed potato around it with your fingers. Smooth the ball so it is round or egg-shaped and roll it in cornstarch.

Deep- or semi-deep-fry the *koftas* in hot oil for 2-3 minutes, until golden brown. Drain well and set aside.

To make the sauce, heat the oil in a pan, add the onions and sauté until softened but not browned. Stir in the ground spices and cook gently for 1-2 minutes. Add the ginger/garlic paste and cook until the garlic gives off its unique aroma. Add the puréed spinach and season with salt. Cook for a minute or two, ensuring that the spinach does not discolor. Now add the fried *koftas* to the sauce. Pour in the cream and heat through gently. Check the seasoning, adding some *garam masala* if you like, and serve.

You can also serve this by placing the hot *koftas* on a platter and pouring the sauce over them or to one side. Do not leave the *koftas* in the sauce if you are not eating them immediately. They will keep in the refrigerator for up to a week if well cooked and tightly covered.

2 large floury potatoes (weighing about one pound in total), peeled and chopped

cornstarch

oil for frying

salt and pepper

For the stuffing:

2 oz paneer or mozzarella

1 heaping tbsp chopped fresh cilantro

2 tsp golden raisins

2 hot green chilies, chopped

2-3 tbsp chopped mixed nuts

For the sauce:

2-3 tbsp oil

2 onions, finely chopped

1 tsp ground cumin

1 tbsp ground coriander

a pinch of ground turmeric

1 tbsp ground dried red chili

1½ tbsp Ginger/Garlic Paste (see page 61)

9 oz fresh spinach, blanched, drained well and puréed

1½ tbsp light cream

2-3 pinches of garam masala (see page 123) (optional)

salt

Illustrated on next page

This unusual dish originally came from Kashmir, although without the potatoes. With a *pulao*, it makes an ideal accompaniment to a rich meat dish such as Khadey Masaley Ka Gosht (see page 62).

Saeb Aur Aloo Ki Subzee

APPLE AND POTATO BHAJEE

2 tbsp oil

a pinch of fenugreek seeds (about 8-10 seeds)

¼ tsp mustard seeds

½ tsp cumin seeds

1 tsp coriander seeds, roasted and lightly crushed (see page 14)

2 hot green chilies

4-5 green onions, including the green part, thinly sliced

2 potatoes, boiled, peeled and cut into ¾-cm cubes

3 cooking apples (not too sour), cored and cut into ¾-cm cubes

1 large tomato, seeded and diced

sugar and lemon juice, to taste (optional)

1 tbsp chopped fresh cilantro

salt

Heat the oil in a wok or large frying pan until hazy. Add the fenugreek seeds and then after 10 seconds or so add the mustard seeds. When they stop crackling, add the cumin and crushed coriander seeds and sauté for about 1½ minutes. Add the green chilies and sauté for a minute. Add the green onions and sauté for 2 minutes, then add the potatoes and apples and toss lightly until well mixed. Add the tomato and cook for 2-3 minutes, tossing occasionally.

As soon as the apples soften slightly, check the seasoning and, if required, add a little sprinkling of sugar and lemon juice and some salt. Sprinkle in the coriander, toss and remove from the heat. Serve immediately.

VARIATION
At the last minute, throw in about 4 oz blanched green beans, cut into tiny pieces. They will add crunch to the dish as well as making it look even brighter.

Khumb Mutter

CREAMY MUSHROOM AND PEA CURRY

Purée all the ingredients for the *masala* to make a smooth, thick paste. Heat the oil in a heavy-bottomed pan, add the cinnamon and sauté for a minute or two over medium heat. Reduce the heat and stir in the *masala*. Increase the heat to medium again and cook, stirring slowly with a wooden spatula, for 5 minutes; take care as the mixture will splatter. Cover and reduce the heat to low. Cook, stirring and scraping the base of the pan every minute or so, until the oil begins to separate out at the edges.

Add enough water to give the consistency of a thick sauce and simmer for about 20 minutes, until the sauce tastes cooked rather than raw. Season with salt, then add the shallots and simmer for a couple of minutes. Add the mushrooms and simmer for 5-6 minutes, until tender, then stir in the peas and tomatoes.

Simmer for 3-4 minutes and then stir in the cream and fresh cilantro. Check the seasoning and serve sprinkled with the pistachios.

VARIATIONS
• The sauce is also suitable for cooking chicken, fish, potatoes and other vegetables.

• Add deep-fried paneer (see page 81) to make a rich, creamy Paneer Khurma.

2 tbsp oil

2-in piece of cinnamon stick

12 shallots, peeled but left whole

2 oz small button mushrooms

7 oz blanched fresh peas (or thawed frozen ones)

10-12 cherry tomatoes

3 tbsp light cream

1 tbsp chopped fresh cilantro

1 tbsp chopped pistachio nuts

salt

For the masala:

1 large onion, coarsely chopped

6 garlic cloves

3/4-in piece of fresh ginger

20 blanched almonds or 3 tbsp ground almonds

3 tbsp broken cashew nuts

3 green cardamom pods

3-4 tbsp Greek-style yogurt

1/2 tsp ground turmeric

1-2 dried red chilies

This is a basic *kadhi* and below are some suggestions for items you can add to it to make a wonderful meal. It is perfect served plain as well. Just enjoy it with rice.

Dahi Kadhi

YOGURT CURRY

SERVES 6

16 oz Greek-style yogurt

2 tbsp oil

1/2 tsp mustard seeds

10-15 curry leaves

1 tsp cumin seeds

1/4 tsp asafetida

3 tbsp besan (chickpea flour), sifted

1/2 tsp ground turmeric

2-3 hot green chilies, slit lengthwise and seeded

5 fl oz water

1 tbsp sugar

1 tbsp chopped fresh cilantro

salt

Put the yogurt in a bowl and whisk until smooth, then set aside.

Heat the oil in a saucepan until it forms a haze and add the mustard seeds. When they stop crackling, add the curry leaves and the cumin. Stir for a minute, being careful not to let the cumin burn, then add the asafetida. Pull the pan off the heat and slowly add the chickpea flour, stirring all the time. Return to low heat and cook, stirring with a wooden spoon. At first the flour will become hard but eventually it will soften and release the oil. At this stage add the turmeric and green chilies and cook for a minute or two longer.

Remove from the heat, let cool for a few minutes, then add the whisked yogurt and mix until you have a smooth paste. (If you add the yogurt over the heat it is likely to become lumpy.) Stir in the water and return to medium heat. Bring to a boil, then add the sugar and some salt. Taste to check the seasoning: it should be slightly sour but also slightly sweet and savory.

Boil for a few minutes until thickened to the consistency of a cream soup. If too thick, dilute to the consistency desired. Add the cilantro and remove from the heat.

VARIATIONS

• Stir some deep-fried okra pieces (see page 118) or fried eggplant into the curry just before serving.

• Add raw sliced okra or raw banana pieces after the curry has come to a boil.

• Add some small onion *bhajias* (see page 10) just before serving.

Aloo Gobi Ki Tahiri

POTATO AND CAULIFLOWER PULAO

Heat the oil in a large saucepan until it forms a haze, then add the mustard seeds. When they stop crackling, reduce the heat slightly and add the green chilies, curry leaves, cumin and lastly the asafetida. As soon as the cumin changes color, stir in the garlic and cook until it begins to turn golden. Add the sliced onions and cook until translucent. Add the turmeric, followed by the potato and cauliflower. Sauté for a minute or two, then pour in the water. Cover and simmer until the potato is half cooked.

Add the rice, sauté for a minute or two, then stir in the lemon juice and enough boiling water to cover the rice by about ¾ in. Cover the pan tightly and simmer very gently, stirring every 2 minutes or so from the bottom up. The rice will fluff up nicely and should be cooked in about 15-20 minutes but if you find that all the water has been absorbed and the rice is still not done, splash a little more water around the edge and in the center, then cover and cook for a few minutes longer.

You can also cook the *pulao* in an oven preheated to 400°F once you have added the boiling water. After 20 minutes, remove from the oven, stir with a two-pronged fork and, if need be, put it back in the oven for a few minutes until the rice is tender.

When cooked, check the seasoning and stir in the cilantro. Serve with yogurt and a light meat or vegetable curry.

5 tbsp oil

¼ tsp mustard seeds

2 hot green chilies, slit lengthwise

8-10 curry leaves

1 tsp cumin seeds

¼ tsp asafetida

6 garlic cloves, chopped

2 onions, finely sliced

¼ tsp ground turmeric

1 large potato, cut into ¾-in cubes

1 small cauliflower, divided into small florets

3 fl oz water

14 oz basmati rice

1 tbsp lemon juice

1 tbsp chopped fresh cilantro

salt

This dish varies from place to place but this is a standard recipe and one that I feel works very well indeed. It makes a lovely accompaniment or starter. The stuffing mixture can also be mixed into yogurt and served as a *raita*.

Bhareli Bhindi

STUFFED OKRA

20-30 okra (choose long, slender ones)

½ tsp ground turmeric

oil for frying

salt

For the stuffing:

4½ oz fresh or frozen grated coconut (see page 96) or 3 oz coconut powder

2 large hot green chilies, finely chopped

1-2 tbsp chopped fresh cilantro

½ tsp coriander seeds, finely crushed but not powdered

½ teaspoon cumin seeds, finely crushed but not powdered

2 tsp chaat masala

Wash the okra and wipe them dry. This is important or they will become gooey when cooked. Slit them open lengthwise and sprinkle the turmeric and some salt inside. Mix together all the ingredients for the stuffing and season lightly. Stuff the okra until they are swollen but do not let them tear.

Pour a thin covering of oil over the bottom of a heavy-bottomed frying pan and sauté the okra, in batches, for about 5 minutes, turning them until golden brown all over. Serve sprinkled with any remaining stuffing and accompanied by thick yogurt.

Thoran

QUICK FRIED BEANS WITH COCONUT

2 tbsp oil

1 tsp mustard seeds

½ onion, finely chopped

3-4 hot green chilies, finely chopped

2-3 tsp dried coconut

¼ tsp ground turmeric

6-8 curry leaves

1 lb green beans, cut into small pieces

salt

Heat the oil in a frying pan until very hot and add the mustard seeds. When they stop crackling, add the onion and green chilies, reduce the heat and cook gently until softened. Stir in the coconut, turmeric, curry leaves and some salt. Then add the beans and 6-8 tablespoons of water. Cover the pan and simmer for a few minutes, then remove the lid and cook, stirring, over low heat until the liquid has evaporated.

VARIATION

This can also be made with cooked *channa daal* (split yellow peas) or lentils, or coarsely chopped fresh spinach or green peas.

Narial Aur Dahi Kay Subz

MIXED VEGETABLES WITH COCONUT

1 onion, sliced

1 potato, peeled and cut into cubes

1 small eggplant, cut into cubes

6-8 okra, cut into ¾-in pieces

1 small green banana, cut into cubes

1 drumstick, stringed and cut into 2-in lengths

1 small snakegourd or a 6-8-in piece, peeled, seeded and cut into cubes

½ tsp ground turmeric

3-4 dried red chilies

2-3 large hot green chilies, chopped

11 oz fresh or frozen grated coconut (see page 96) or 7 oz dried coconut

½ tsp cumin seeds

7 fl oz Greek-style yogurt

salt

For the tempering:

2 tbsp coconut oil

½ tsp mustard seeds

15 curry leaves

Put all the vegetables in a large pan, add the turmeric, red chilies and some salt, then pour in enough water just to cover the vegetables. Simmer until they are half cooked.

Grind together the green chilies, coconut and cumin seeds in a blender. When the cumin is well ground, add the yogurt and whirl briefly. Add this mixture to the vegetables and bring slowly back to a boil, stirring constantly. Cook until the vegetables are completely tender. (This is how they are enjoyed in India but you could keep them slightly crunchy if you prefer.)

For the tempering, heat the coconut oil in a frying pan until hazy, then add the mustard seeds and curry leaves. When the mustard seeds stop crackling, pour this mixture into the vegetables, stir well, then check the seasoning. Serve with plain steamed rice or with crumpets – these can be steamed briefly to heat them and are perfect for soaking up the juices.

TEMPERING (*BAGHAAR* OR *VAGHAAR*)

Tempering is the term used to describe a last-minute flavoring of whole spices quickly fried in oil and then poured on to a finished dish to give it a final touch of glory. It is particularly common in the vegetarian cooking of the Gujerat and southern India and is almost always added to *daals* (lentil preparations). Although tempering is done primarily to add flavor, medicinal considerations are important too, as is often the case in Indian cooking. So the tempering for lentil dishes traditionally consists of spices that are well-known anti-flatulents, such as asafetida, cumin and mustard.

Tempering is a very simple way of enlivening basic ingredients. Thus, if you were to boil, peel and cut up some potatoes and then pour over them some very hot oil to which has been added mustard seeds, cumin seeds, asafetida and curry leaves, you have just tempered the potato and can call it *aloo bhaji*.

This can be served as a side dish or on its own with corn tortillas. In the north of India, where corn grows in abundance, a great many breads are made from corn. Instead of tortillas we eat corn *papads*, better known in England and elsewhere as *papadums*.

Gobi Aur Makki Kay Daney

CAULIFLOWER COOKED WITH CORN

7 oz fresh or thawed frozen corn

1 tsp cumin seeds

2 tsp coriander seeds

3 tbsp oil

1 onion, chopped

1 tbsp Ginger/Garlic Paste (see page 61)

2 hot green chilies, chopped

1 small cauliflower, divided into small florets

2 tomatoes, chopped

2-3 heaping tbsp Greek-style yogurt

2 tbsp chopped fresh cilantro

salt

If you are using fresh corn, cook it in boiling salted water until tender, then drain and set aside.

Lightly roast the cumin and coriander seeds in a small dry frying pan, then crush them in a mortar.

Heat the oil in a pan, add the onion and sauté lightly over medium heat until just about to brown. Add the ginger/garlic paste and green chilies and sauté for 2 minutes, then stir in the crushed coriander and cumin and sauté for a minute or two longer. Add the corn and cook for a minute, then stir in the cauliflower florets and sauté for another 4-5 minutes. Put in half a cup of water and some salt and simmer until the cauliflower is half cooked. Do not overcook. Add the tomatoes and cook for a minute or two.

When the cauliflower is just tender, beat the yogurt with a fork or a small whisk until smooth and add to the mixture. Simmer uncovered for 4-5 minutes, until you have a rich, creamy-looking sauce. Check the seasoning, sprinkle in the fresh cilantro and serve.

VARIATION
Garnish with shredded green or red chili and ginger. If you have some browned onions set aside, these will also add a great touch. Coarsely chopped roasted unsalted peanuts may be mixed with the cilantro for extra flavor.

Potatoes are a great favorite in India and are cooked in a variety of ways. This recipe is very simple and easy to follow.

Aloo Ki Subzee

SPICED POTATOES

Heat a layer of oil in a large, heavy-bottomed pan until it forms a haze. Add the mustard seeds, cumin seeds, curry leaves, asafetida and green chilies and cook until the mustard seeds stop crackling. Add the onions and sauté until softened but not colored, then add the potatoes. Sauté until the potatoes are evenly coated in the oil and spices, then stir in the ground spices, some salt and enough water to just about half cover the potatoes. Cover the pan with a tight-fitting lid and simmer over low heat, stirring from time to time so the potatoes cook evenly. When the potatoes are almost done, add the tomatoes. Cook uncovered until the potatoes are tender and the sauce has thickened. Check the seasoning, stir in the cilantro and serve.

VARIATION
You could also mix in some green peas at the end for a colorful finish.

oil for frying

$1/2$ tsp mustard seeds

1 tsp cumin seeds

8-10 curry leaves

$1/4$ tsp asafetida

2 long hot green chilies, cut into 2-3 pieces each

14 oz onions, finely sliced

$1^1/2$ lb potatoes, peeled and diced

$1/2$ tsp ground turmeric

$1/2$ tsp ground dried red chili

1 tsp ground coriander

$1/2$ tsp ground cumin

9 oz tomatoes, chopped

1 tbsp chopped fresh cilantro

salt

A recipe from the Saraswat Brahmins of the Konkan. You will need to find unripe green mangoes for this. However, some of the red-skinned South American mangoes are very firm and could be substituted for green ones, although the flavor will be slightly different. If you use fresh coconut, you may like to garnish the finished dish with a few shavings, frying them in the oil before adding the mustard seeds, etc. (see page 106).

Aambey Chi Udda Methi

GREEN MANGOES WITH FENUGREEK AND JAGGERY

9 oz fresh or frozen grated coconut (see below) or 5 oz coconut powder

4-6 large dried red chilies

½ tsp fenugreek seeds

½ tsp ground turmeric

2 tbsp oil

½ tsp mustard seeds

2 tsp urad daal (white split gram beans)

15 curry leaves

¼ tsp asafetida

2-4 green mangoes, depending on size, peeled, pitted and cut into thin slivers

1½-2 oz jaggery

1 tbsp chopped fresh cilantro (optional)

salt

Grind the coconut with the red chilies, fenugreek seeds and turmeric, then set aside.

Heat the oil in a pan until very hot. Test the heat by throwing in a few mustard seeds; they should crackle. When the oil is hot enough, add the rest of the mustard seeds, the white split gram beans, curry leaves and asafetida. Once the gram beans have turned golden brown and give off a lovely nutty aroma, stir in the ground coconut mixture and sauté for a couple of minutes. Add the mangoes and a cup of water and simmer for 10-15 minutes, until the mangoes are almost tender. Put in the jaggery and simmer for a few minutes until the mixture has thickened. Taste and add salt if necessary. Stir in the cilantro, if using.

TO PREPARE FRESH COCONUT
Where recipes call for grated coconut, dried coconut will not do. Instead buy a packet of frozen grated coconut, sold in Indian food markets, or buy a whole coconut and grate your own. Wet the coconut thoroughly and then mark a line all around the circumference with your fingers. Hold the coconut in one hand (over a bowl to catch the liquid) and hit it along the line with the back of a cleaver to crack it open; keep turning the coconut to work all round it. Drain out the liquid, then cut the flesh away from the shell with a sharp knife and peel off the skin. Grate the flesh on the fine side of a grater (or use a special coconut grater). One coconut should yield about 9 oz.

Foogath derives from the Portuguese *refogado*, a thick onion purée which forms the basis of many slow-cooked Portuguese dishes. This Goan recipe has strayed a long way from its European origins and is more like a stir-fry. Green beans can be used instead of carrots.

Cabbage and Carrot Foogath

Heat the oil in a large heavy-bottomed saucepan over high heat until a haze forms, then add the mustard seeds. When they stop crackling, reduce the heat to medium and add the curry leaves, cumin and red chilies. Sauté for a minute, then stir in the onions. When the onions turn soft, add the garlic and sauté for a minute or two, then stir in the turmeric, followed by the cabbage. Sauté the cabbage for a minute or two, then add the coconut. Sauté for 4–5 minutes, then mix in the carrots and check the seasoning. Cook for 2 minutes only; the carrots should still be crunchy. Sprinkle in a few drops of lime juice and add the cilantro. Cover the pan, remove from the heat and let stand for 4–5 minutes.

Serve as an accompaniment or simply with hot crusty rolls.

2 tbsp oil

$\frac{1}{4}$ tsp mustard seeds

10 curry leaves

$\frac{1}{2}$ tsp cumin seeds

2 dried red chilies, cut into $\frac{1}{2}$-in pieces

2 onions, thinly sliced

6–8 garlic cloves, chopped

$\frac{1}{4}$ tsp ground turmeric

9–11 oz white cabbage, shredded

9 oz fresh or frozen grated coconut (see opposite)

9 oz carrots, cut into thin strips

lime juice, to taste

1 tbsp chopped fresh cilantro

salt

There are several different ways of preparing this Parsee dish. However, this is a simplified version, which I particularly enjoy. It makes a great side dish. Some Parsees like to add a little tamarind.

Bhaji Nay Dana Ma Kolmi

SPINACH COOKED WITH GREEN PEAS AND SHRIMP

1 lb shelled raw shrimp

½ tsp ground turmeric

1 tbsp lemon juice

2-3 tbsp oil

6-8 garlic cloves, chopped

1 tsp cumin seeds, roasted and lightly crushed (see page 14)

2 onions, finely chopped

2-in piece of fresh ginger, chopped

2 hot green chilies, seeded and chopped

9 oz fresh spinach, finely shredded

3-4 heaping tbsp cooked green peas

1 tsp sugar (optional)

1-1½ tbsp chopped fresh cilantro

salt

Wash the shrimp and then drain thoroughly. Place them in a bowl and mix with the turmeric and lemon juice.

Heat the oil in a large pan. Add the garlic and crushed cumin seeds and sauté for a minute or two, stirring, until the garlic is pale golden. Add the onions, ginger and green chilies and sauté until the onions are pale brown. Add the spinach and increase the heat to high. Sauté for a minute or two, then add the peas and swirl for a minute until they are hot. Add the shrimp and some salt. Mix in briefly but do not stir too much or the shrimp will give off their juices.

After a couple of minutes, when the shrimp are almost cooked, add the sugar if you like, and the chopped cilantro. Check the seasoning and remove from the heat. Cover and let sit for a few minutes so the shrimp finish cooking in the heat of the pan.

Fansi Jeera Tamatarwala

GREEN BEANS WITH CUMIN AND TOMATOES

Heat the oil in a large frying pan, add the garlic, onion and cumin and sauté for a minute or two over medium heat. Add the ground chili. When the onion turns opaque, increase the heat to high and add the beans. Cook for 2–3 minutes, tossing them occasionally, then sprinkle with salt and add the tomatoes. Toss for a minute or so, then check the seasoning, add the fresh cilantro, if you like, and remove from the heat. It's important not to let the beans overcook; they should be slightly crunchy. If water seeps out of them, it means the heat was too low.

Sprinkle over some *chaat masala* or a little ground cumin before serving.

2 tbsp oil

3–4 garlic cloves, finely chopped

1 onion, finely chopped

1 tsp cumin seeds, roasted and lightly crushed (see page 14)

$^{1}/_{4}$ tsp ground red chili

9 oz slender green beans, trimmed

2 tomatoes, seeded and chopped

1 tbsp chopped fresh cilantro (optional)

salt

chaat masala or ground cumin, for serving

Illustrated on page 109

Rice, Legumes
and Breads

These simple croquettes can be made from left-over boiled rice. In Goa they are rolled in semolina instead of bread crumbs, which gives a lovely crunchy texture. Serve with Fresh Tomato Chutney (see page 119).

Fofos De Arroz

RICE AND CHEESE CROQUETTES

Mix the cheese with the cilantro, green chilies and paprika or ground chili.

Season the rice with a little salt and mash it a bit with the palms of your hands until it is soft enough to be shaped. Shape into 8 balls. Take each one in the palm of your hand, flatten it, place some of the cheese mixture in the center and then pull the rice around it, making sure the filling is completely covered. Form into a cylinder shape and then roll in the flour. Dip the croquettes into the beaten egg and then into the bread crumbs. At this stage, they can be kept, covered, in the refrigerator overnight if necessary.

To cook, heat enough oil in a frying pan to give a depth of about ¾ in. Add the croquettes and fry until golden brown all over. Drain on paper towels and serve.

4 tbsp grated Cheddar cheese

1½ tbsp chopped fresh cilantro

2 hot green chilies, chopped

1 tsp paprika or ground dried red chili

9 oz rice, boiled and cooled

3-4 tbsp all-purpose flour

2 eggs, beaten

dried bread crumbs for coating

oil for frying

salt

Pulao, pilav, palav and *pilaf* - however it is spelled it is basically the same dish: rice seasoned with a little oil and flavorings, then cooked. However, there are several regional and domestic variations. The recipe I give here is very simple and, hopefully, foolproof. Don't worry if you do spoil your rice; you can make croquettes with it the next day (see Fofos de Arroz on page 101).

Pulao

1 lb basmati or other good long grain rice

3 tbsp oil or ghee

2-in piece of cinnamon stick

2-3 cardamom pods

2-3 cloves

1 tsp cumin seeds

salt

Wash the rice in cold water and drain. Heat the oil or *ghee* in a heavy-bottomed saucepan about 10 inches in diameter. Add the whole spices and fry for a minute or two until they swell and change color. Add the rice and sauté for 2-3 minutes, stirring so that all the grains get evenly heated.

At this stage you must have a kettle of hot water ready. Rice normally absorbs three times its volume of water, so for 1 lb of rice you will need about 50 fl oz of water. However, the level of absorption can vary depending on the brand, so I recommend that you add just 35 fl oz of water to begin with. Stir well, dislodging any grains of rice from the side of the pan, add some salt and bring to a boil. Reduce the heat, cover and cook gently for about 15 minutes, until the rice is tender but still slightly firm. Stir every minute or so at first. If the water is absorbed too rapidly, add a little more but be careful not to make the rice too wet. Once it is done, loosen the grains with a fork, then cover and set aside until needed.

You can finish the rice in the oven if you prefer. After it has been simmering for 7-8 minutes, transfer it to an oven preheated to 375°F and bake for about 15-20 minutes. You probably won't need to add any more water in this case. If the rice is mushy (and this happens to the best of us occasionally), you can return it to the oven to dry out.

TIP
Always crack cardamom pods open before frying; this gives a better flavor and also prevents them from exploding in the heat of the pan.

This is perhaps my favorite dish when served with a masala-fried fish. Parsee in origin, it is simple to make, nutritious, wholesome and, above all, delicious. The *vaghaar*, or tempering, is the final touch to a simple masterpiece, and can be used for other types of lentils, chickpeas etc.

Dhan Daar Nay Vaghaar

PURÉED LENTILS WITH RICE AND FRIED ONIONS

Add the turmeric to the lentils and their soaking water and bring to a boil. Add some salt, reduce the heat and simmer, removing any scum from the top, for 30 minutes or until very tender. Stir in the butter and then purée the lentils and their liquid to a smooth paste with the consistency of a thick pouring sauce.

For the *vaghaar*, put the butter and oil in a small pan and heat slowly. Add the cumin seeds and then, 30 seconds later, the chopped garlic. Cook gently, stirring, until the garlic is golden brown, adding the chili half way through, if using. Add to the puréed *daal*.

For the rice, bring a pan of approximately 1.5-2 litres of water to a boil with the bay leaves, cardamom and some salt. Add the rice and stir, then simmer for 8-10 minutes, until the rice is cooked but still slightly firm. Drain well and keep warm.

Finally, prepare the fried onions. Heat the oil in a pan over medium-high heat and add the onions. Stir them gently but frequently until they begin to turn light brown. At this point you will notice that oil is oozing out again and the onions are actually frying. This is a crucial stage: if you neglect them they will burn. Reduce the heat to low and keep stirring, breaking up any lumps and making sure that the onions stay beneath the oil. Have a sieve placed over a bowl (not a plastic one) and a fork kept handy. As soon as you see the onions turning a darker shade of brown, drain them into the sieve and loosen them with the fork, separating all the strands. If you don't do this the onions will continue cooking in the sieve and turn black. They have a unique way of holding hot oil and can burn very quickly.

Before serving, reheat the rice if necessary, and heat the lentils very gently, stirring with a wooden spoon or spatula and scraping the bottom of the pan. Mix in the chopped cilantro. Serve the lentils on the rice, topped with the fried onions.

1 tsp ground turmeric

7 oz toover daal (yellow lentils), washed well, then soaked in water to cover by ½ in for 2-3 hours

½ oz butter

1 tbsp chopped fresh cilantro

salt

For the vaghaar:

½ oz butter

1 tbsp oil

1 tsp cumin seeds

8-10 garlic cloves, coarsely chopped

1 green chili, cut lengthwise into quarters (optional)

For the rice:

2 bay leaves

2 green cardamom pods

salt

14 oz basmati rice

For the fried onions:

4-5 tbsp oil

2 onions, finely sliced

Ragda is a Gujerati dish of dried white peas, served with *pattice* or *poorie* (see pages 24 and 25). It can also be eaten as a side dish with rice. Use *channa daal* (split yellow peas) if you prefer, as they are more readily available.

When you are boiling beans or lentils, skim off the scum on the top as often as necessary, unless you are using a pressure cooker.

Ragda

CURRIED WHITE PEAS

7 oz watana (dried white peas), soaked overnight and then drained

a pinch of baking soda

3-4 tbsp oil

1 tsp cumin seeds

1 tbsp chopped fresh ginger

1 tbsp chopped garlic

2 green chilies, chopped

2 onions, chopped

¼ tsp ground turmeric

1 tsp ground dried red chili

2 tbsp chopped fresh cilantro

salt

Put the white peas in a pan with the baking soda and some salt. Add just enough water to cover and then simmer until soft, topping up with a little more water if necessary. Drain the peas and reserve the cooking liquid.

Heat the oil in a large pan, add the cumin and sauté for 1-2 minutes without letting it burn. Add the ginger, garlic and green chilies and sauté for a minute or so, or until the garlic changes color slightly. Add the onions and cook until soft and translucent. Mix in the turmeric and ground chili and sauté for a minute or so, then stir in the boiled peas. Heat through and check the seasoning. Add the cooking liquid and cook for a few minutes until the mixture has a mushy texture. Stir in the chopped cilantro and serve.

In the Punjab and Pakistan this traditional dish is served on most festive occasions. It is also very good with fried *paneer* stirred in.

Choley Pindi

PUNJABI-STYLE CHICKPEAS

If using soaked dried chickpeas, put them in a pan with enough fresh water to cover by about ¾ in and boil until tender. Drain and set aside.

Heat the oil in a heavy-bottomed pan, add the cumin and sauté for a minute without letting it burn. Add the onion, then the garlic, ginger and green chilies, and cook until the onion is softened. Stir in the tomatoes, followed by the yogurt. Add the chickpeas and cook, stirring frequently, until the mixture is thoroughly heated through. Add the *masala*, if using, or squeeze in a few drops of lemon juice, then stir in the cilantro. Season to taste with salt and serve with *bhaturas*, *poories* or *parathas*.

VARIATION
If you can find them, gently roast and powder 2 tablespoons of pomegranate seeds. Sprinkle over before serving.

7 oz kabuli channa (chickpeas), soaked overnight and then drained, or 14-oz can of chickpeas, drained

2–3 tbsp oil

2 tsp cumin seeds, crushed

1 onion, finely chopped

5–6 garlic cloves, finely chopped

¾-in piece of fresh ginger, chopped

2–3 green chilies, slit lengthwise

2 tomatoes, chopped

4 tbsp Greek-style yogurt

1 tsp channa masala or chaat masala, if available, or a squeeze of lemon juice

2 tbsp chopped fresh cilantro

salt

Illustrated on page 108

This is often eaten for breakfast with a crusty roll in parts of Maharashtra and Goa.

Watana Ussal

CHICKPEAS WITH COCONUT

9 oz watana (white chickpeas), or other dried white peas if you prefer, soaked overnight and then drained

5 tbsp oil

3 onions, sliced

9 oz fresh or frozen grated coconut (see page 96) or 5 oz coconut powder

6-8 dried red chilies

2 tsp coriander seeds

1 tsp cumin seeds

½ tsp ground turmeric

6-8 cloves

6-8 black peppercorns

1 tbsp white poppy seeds

1 tsp mustard seeds

12-15 curry leaves

1-2 tbsp chopped fresh cilantro (optional)

fried fresh coconut, to garnish (see right)

salt

Put the drained peas in a pan with enough water to cover them by about ¾ in and boil until tender. Drain and set aside.

Heat half the oil in a heavy-bottomed pan, add the onions and cook gently until light brown. Add the coconut and continue to cook until the coconut is brown. The mixture will stick to the pan, so it is important to use a heavy pan and to keep stirring and scraping the bottom with a wooden spoon. Stir in the chilies, coriander and cumin seeds, turmeric, cloves, peppercorns and poppy seeds and sauté for a few minutes over low heat. Let cool, then grind the mixture to a thick paste, adding just a little water if using a blender.

Heat the remaining oil in a separate pan until very hot – test it by adding a few mustard seeds: they should crackle. Once the oil is hot enough, add all the mustard seeds to the pan. When they stop crackling, add the curry leaves and then stir in the spice paste. Sauté for about 2 minutes, then stir in the peas and enough of their cooking liquid to give a porridgy consistency. Taste and adjust the seasoning. Stir in the fresh cilantro, if using, and garnish with fried fresh coconut.

TO FRY FRESH COCONUT
Make shavings of the coconut flesh on a mandoline or grater or with a vegetable peeler, then sauté them in about 1 tablespoon of oil, stirring, until golden.

There can be no definitive recipe for *chapatis*. It is only through experience that you learn to judge the consistency of the dough and to roll it out deftly. When you attempt to produce smooth, round chapatis and end up plotting the world in different shapes, remember that even chefs and people such as myself with 20 years' experience cannot roll them out as skilfully as our mothers or wives. In hotels and restaurants throughout India where you see chapatis on the menu there is always a specialist employed. However, if you follow this recipe you will end up with a tasty bread that makes a good accompaniment to all sorts of foods, even if it is not perfectly shaped. Good luck.

Chapatis

MAKES 10-12

**9 oz whole wheat flour
or medium chapati flour**

1 tsp salt

1 tbsp oil, warmed

melted ghee or oil, for frying

Illustrated on previous pages:
Choley Pindi *(see page 105)*
and Fansi Jeera Tamatarwala
(see page 99)

Sift the flour and salt into a bowl and stir in the oil. Gradually stir in enough cold water to give a firm dough, then turn out and knead for about 5 minutes, until the dough is no longer sticky. Cover with a bowl or plastic wrap and set aside for an hour or two.

Divide the dough into 10-12 balls. Place each one on a lightly floured surface and flatten slightly with the palm of your hand. Then roll out into a round no more than $\frac{1}{8}$ in thick.

Heat a *tawa* or flat griddle, pour in about a teaspoon of melted *ghee* or oil and swirl to coat (or use a pastry brush). Dust off any excess flour from the *chapati* and place it on the pan. After about 30 seconds, flip it over with a spatula and brush the top with *ghee* or oil. Cook for another 30 seconds, then flip it over again and brush the other side with fat (this is the Parsee style. The Gujeratis and several other Indian communities do not add *ghee* or butter till the very end.) When the *chapati* is cooked through, fold it in half, place in a container lined with paper towel or cheesecloth and cover with a lid.

A good *chapati* is one that is cooked through but not burnt. If the pan is too hot, the *chapati* will brown instantly. You will probably get some brown spots on it in any case, which is fine unless you are a young Gujerati bride demonstrating your cooking skills to your future in-laws.

Vegetables can be included in the dough for *rotis* and *parathas*, adding flavor and giving them a distinct character. An entire chapter could be written on Indian breads but here is one simple variation on the basic dough.

Mooli Aur Pyaz Ki Roti

WHITE RADISH AND ONION ROTI

Sift the flour and salt into a bowl, stir in the warm oil, then knead in all the remaining ingredients with your hands so they release some of their juices into the flour. Gradually add enough cold water to make a firm dough. Turn out and knead for about 5 minutes, so the dough is well flavored with the vegetables. If they are particularly moist and the dough gets sticky, knead in a little more flour. Cover the dough with a bowl and set aside for about half an hour.

Slowly heat a *tawa* or flat griddle but don't let it get too hot or the *rotis* will brown before they are cooked through. Divide the dough into 8 balls. Dip the tips of your fingers in oil and press down firmly on each ball to flatten it. Sprinkle with a little flour (combined with the oil, this gives a nice crisp coating). On a lightly floured surface, roll out each ball into a round about $1/4$ in thick - any thinner and it will probably crack because of the vegetables. Dust off any excess flour from the surface. Brush the griddle with oil and slap the *roti* on to it. After about 30 seconds, when it is beginning to loosen from the base of the pan, flip it over with a spatula and then sprinkle the top with a little oil. Cook for another 30 seconds or so, then flip it over again and sprinkle the other side with oil. When the *roti* is cooked through, place it in container lined with paper towel or muslin and cover with a lid.

MAKES 8

9 oz whole wheat flour or medium chapati flour

1 tsp salt

1 tbsp oil, warmed, plus oil for frying

1 small white radish (mooli), peeled and finely grated

1 onion, very finely chopped

1 tbsp chopped fresh cilantro

1 small green chili, finely chopped

Dips, Raitas, Chutneys and Pickles

Bapaiji, meaning paternal grandmother, is what my kids call my mother. This superb mayonnaise is made in a blender with whole eggs and is quite foolproof. It has always worked for me and for all the chefs who have trained under me. My mother taught me how to make it when I was just 12 years old. In India we keep it in small jars in the refrigerator for months on end. Mayonnaise is used quite a lot in Indian cooking, for parties and festive occasions. There is an Indian version of Russian salad made with vegetables, pineapple and mayonnaise.

Bapaiji Todiwala's Homemade Mayonnaise

Put all the ingredients except the oil in a blender and process on medium speed for about a minute. Put the oil into a container with a lip so it will be easy to pour. Start the machine again and pour in the oil through the hole in the lid in a slow trickle. After 2 fl oz or so of oil have gone in, you can add it a little more quickly. Stop after a minute to check that the mayonnaise is blending well. Make sure that the blender container is not heating up. If this happens, you will have to stop for a while and remove the lid to allow rapid cooling. Continue adding the oil until you see that the well in the middle of the mayonnaise has closed up. At this stage, stop the machine, remove the container and give it a shake until the air bubble trapped inside bursts. Start the machine again and pour in more oil; you will see that a small well has started to appear again. Add the oil slowly until the well disappears or the machine begins to whine. Stop and shake the container again. Keep doing this until the well no longer forms after shaking. Your mayonnaise is now ready. If you are satisfied with the consistency before this stage is reached you can stop earlier. However, the more oil the eggs absorb, the longer the mayonnaise will keep.

Taste and adjust the seasoning, adding more lime juice and salt if necessary. Whisk them in either by hand in a bowl or by giving the mayonnaise another quick whirl in the blender.

2 eggs

2 tsp good-quality coarse grain mustard

$^3/_4$ tsp salt

$^3/_4$ tsp sugar

$1^1/_2$ tsp Worcestershire sauce

$1^1/_2$ tsp lime juice

$^1/_4$ tsp freshly ground pepper

about 8 fl oz unflavored oil, such as sunflower

TIP
Use cold eggs and, if possible, cool the oil a little bit in the refrigerator until it gets cloudy but not too thick.

Yogurt Chutney Dip

Prepare one quantity of the Green Coconut Chutney on page 36. Mix with thick yogurt until you are happy with the flavor. You may need to thin it with a few drops of lemon juice or water. Stir in 1 finely chopped seeded hot green chili, some finely diced seeded cucumber, a pinch of sugar and some chopped fresh cilantro to taste.

Yogurt, Tamarind and Chili Dip

Mix 4 oz Greek-style yogurt with 1-2 tablespoons tamarind paste and 1 seeded and finely chopped hot green chili. Stir in 1½ teaspoons chopped fresh cilantro, 1 teaspoon finely chopped fresh dill and 1 very finely chopped garlic clove. Season with 1 teaspoon sugar and some ground dried red chili and salt to taste.

Serve this with all sorts of snacks. It goes particularly well with smoked meats.

Mango Chutney Dip

Place all the ingredients in a blender and purée until smooth. It keeps indefinitely in a jar in the refrigerator.

9-oz jar of sweet mango chutney

5-6 garlic cloves

¾-in piece of fresh ginger

2-3 hot green chilies

This is a simple version of a classic Maharashtrian-style chutney. You can buy roasted peanuts or, for a better flavor, roast your own by placing them in a low oven until the skin flakes off.

Hot and Spicy Garlic and Peanut Chutney

The best way to make this is to grind all the ingredients together in a mortar and pestle until you have a thick, fairly smooth paste. Alternatively grind them in a blender, adding the oil a little at a time and scraping down the sides of the blender with a spatula with each addition.

15-20 garlic cloves

7 oz lightly roasted peanuts

6-8 large dried red chilies

oil

salt

Illustrated on the next page: a selection of dips, raitas, chutneys and pickles

Raita

A *raita*, or *raitha*, is made by adding spices and chopped vegetables or fruit to yogurt. The usual spices are ground dried red chili, ground cumin, *chaat masala* and salt. You can make *raitas* with finely diced seeded cucumber, onion, tomato, boiled potato, boiled rice – and even crisply fried Chinese egg noodles, though they must be added just before serving. Fruits such as apple, orange, plum and papaya are all suitable – use your imagination to come up with interesting combinations. It is essential to use good thick yogurt for *raitas*, and don't forget to add plenty of chopped fresh cilantro.

Serve *raitas* as a condiment with semi-dry Indian dishes. They also make excellent dips for *poories*, *chapatis*, etc., and are very soothing for upset stomachs.

Deep-fried okra is very popular with the Parsee community. This delicious deep-fried okra raita is a bit time-consuming to prepare but very easy.

CRISPY OKRA RAITA

oil for frying
7 oz okra, trimmed and finely sliced
4 oz Greek-style yogurt
chaat masala
ground dried red chili
chopped fresh cilantro
salt

Pour enough oil into a wok to fill it to a depth of ³⁄₄ in. Place over medium heat, being careful not to let it get too hot. To test the temperature, throw in a couple of slices of okra; if they brown in less than a minute, reduce the heat and wait a minute or two. Fry the okra (in small batches so that you can control the browning) until it is deep brown but not burnt – this will take about 3-4 minutes. The okra will absorb a lot of oil and then release it. Drain thoroughly in a colander or sieve and let cool.

Mix the yogurt with *chaat masala*, ground chili, fresh cilantro and salt to taste. Mix in the crispy okra at the very last minute before serving, sprinkling some over the top as a garnish, too.

Although this is a fresh chutney, the seasoning acts as a mild preservative. It also adds flavor. The chutney will keep for up to 10 days in the refrigerator if well sealed.

Fresh Tomato Chutney

Put the tomatoes, chilies, garlic, *chaat masala* and cilantro in a glass or metal bowl and mix well, adding salt to taste. For the seasoning, heat the oil in a frying pan until a haze forms and then add the mustard seeds. When they stop crackling, add the curry leaves, then the cumin and lastly the asafetida. Immediately stir this into the chutney. It should make a hissing sound.

4-5 tomatoes, skinned, seeded and chopped

1-2 green chilies, very finely chopped

2-3 garlic cloves, very finely chopped

1 tsp chaat masala

1 tbsp chopped fresh cilantro

salt

For the seasoning:

3 tbsp oil

$\frac{1}{4}$ tsp mustard seeds

6-8 curry leaves, shredded

1 tsp cumin seeds

a pinch of asafetida, if available

My sister-in-law often prepares this simple chili pickle and it is always very popular. You can also make it with fresh red chilies or try vegetables such as carrot, rutabaga, turnip or beet.

Mami June Nu Marcha Nu Achaar

AUNTIE JUNE'S GREEN CHILI PICKLE

16 oz large green chilies

8 fl oz mustard oil

2 tbsp coarse-grain mustard

2 tbsp salt

1 tsp ground turmeric

1/4 tsp asafetida

10-12 garlic cloves, peeled and cut lengthwise into quarters

2 tbsp lemon juice

Wash the chilies and let dry, then remove the stalks and cut the chilies into 1/2-in pieces. Heat the mustard oil to smoking point and then let sit until warm.

Put the chilies into a large bowl and mix in the mustard, salt, turmeric, asafetida and garlic. Add the warm oil and mix in well. Transfer to a large sterilized preserving jar, tie a piece of cheesecloth over the top and leave for a day or two. Then seal the jar tightly and place it on a windowsill where it will catch at least a little sunlight. Leave it for a month, or for 2 weeks if there is plenty of sun.

As long as the level of the oil in the jar is well above the chilies, the pickle should last for a very long time. Wipe the sides with a tissue each time you remove some chilies.

This traditional Goan dish can be served as a starter or stored and used as a condiment with curry or rice dishes.

Balchao De Camarao

PICKLED SHRIMP GOAN STYLE

Wash the shrimp, sprinkle with a little salt and set aside.

Pour a thin layer of oil over the bottom of a heavy pan (if you are going to keep the *balchao* as a pickle it is essential to have some extra oil to act as a preservative). Heat the oil, add the onions and sauté, stirring frequently, until a deep golden brown. Be careful not to burn them but let them get as dark as possible. Add the curry leaves and then the *masala* and continue cooking until the oil has separated out from the *masala*.

Heat a little oil in a heavy-bottomed frying pan until very, very hot. Drain the shrimp thoroughly and put them in the pan, standing well back in case they splatter. Level them out but do not stir immediately or the oil will cool down and the shrimp will release their moisture, thereby boiling instead of sautéing. As soon as the shrimp are cooked and any liquid has dried, stir them into the *masala* and onions and simmer for a couple of minutes. Check the seasoning and stir in the shrimp powder.

Let cool, then transfer to sterilized jars and place in the refrigerator, uncovered. When chilled, seal the jars. If you are using very small shrimp, the pickle will not need refrigerating. Large ones, however, will contain some moisture, which will contaminate the pickle if not refrigerated.

TO SERVE AS A STARTER
Either use shrimp *balchao* on its own or add some other shellfish to it, such as mussels, clams etc. Heat a little oil from the balchao in a pan and, if using shellfish, sauté them over high heat for a few minutes. Add some chopped tomatoes and then stir in *balchao* to taste. Cook until saucelike, then sprinkle with fresh cilantro and check the seasoning. Serve on toasted ciabatta bread.

14 oz shelled raw shrimp

oil for frying

6 onions, finely chopped

15 curry leaves

2 tbsp Piri-piri Masala (see page 123)

2 tsp shrimp powder

salt

A simple venison pickle that can be eaten fresh or stored for later use. If you like a bit of punch, add some slit green chilies just before frying the cooked venison.

Haran Nu Achaar

VENISON PICKLE

1 lb venison, finely diced

1 tsp ground turmeric

10 cloves

2 tbsp lemon juice

15-20 garlic cloves, peeled and cut into quarters lengthwise

7 fl oz oil

3 onions, finely sliced

7 oz jaggery

1 tsp ground cumin

1 tbsp ground coriander

1 tbsp ground dried red chili

1-1½ tbsp salt, to taste

Place the venison in a large pot, cover with enough water to come about ¼ in above the meat and bring to a boil. Add the turmeric, cloves, lemon juice and garlic. Reduce the heat and simmer for 20 minutes.

Meanwhile, heat the oil in a heavy-bottomed pan and deep-fry the onions (in 2 or 3 batches) until deep brown. Stir them regularly and do not let them sit at the bottom of the pan for long. As soon as the onions are light golden, start transferring them to a sieve set over a bowl. By the time you have removed them all, they will be brown and will continue to brown in the sieve. Loosen any clumps with a fork and allow to drain well.

When the venison has been cooking for 20 minutes, add the jaggery. Continue cooking until the excess liquid has evaporated and the meat is lightly coated, then remove from the heat.

Reheat the oil from frying the onions, adding any oil from the bowl below the drained onions. Add the cooked venison to the oil, then almost at once add the cumin, coriander and ground chili. Cook for a minute or two and add the onions. Mix well and check the seasoning. Put into hot sterilized jars immediately and seal. Ideally the pickle should be left to stand for at least a week before eating. You can, however, eat it right away as a condiment.

TIP
To sterilize preserving jars, wash them in a dishwasher if you have one. Alternatively, wash them in hot water, then microwave on high for 3 minutes. If you do not have a microwave put the jars (with their lids open) in a large pan with just enough water to keep them stable. Simmer for 15-20 minutes.

Piri-piri Masala

This is the classic Goan red *masala* and is one of the most versatile spice pastes in Indian cooking. It is equally useful with seafood, white meat and pork but it is not often used with red meats. If you cannot get palm vinegar, use cider vinegar instead.

Put the chilies, ginger, garlic and spices in a bowl, pour over the vinegar to cover, then cover tightly and set aside for at least 3 hours, preferably overnight. Grind to a smooth paste. If using a blender you may need more vinegar. Add it a little at a time, taking care not to make the paste runny.

This paste will keep indefinitely in a sterilized Mason jar in the refrigerator. After using some of the *masala*, pour a spoonful of oil over the top of the remainder to prevent it from drying out. If it does begin to look dry, add a little vinegar from time to time to revive it. Make sure that you wipe the sides of the jar clean with a tissue each time the level drops.

7 oz large dried red chilies, broken or snipped into pieces

2 oz fresh ginger, coarsely sliced

10 garlic cloves, coarsely sliced

1 tbsp coriander seeds

1 tsp cumin seeds

2-in piece of cinnamon stick

5-6 peppercorns

about 7 fl oz palm vinegar or cider vinegar

Garam Masala

Garam means hot and so *garam masala* is literally a hot spice mix. It is usually added to dishes at the last minute as a flavoring, rather than cooked at the beginning like a *masala* paste. Most chefs have their own recipe, which they guard fiercely, but the most common spices are cinnamon, cardamom, cloves, peppercorns, cumin, nutmeg, mace, star anise and coriander. The whole spices are roasted slowly, then ground and stored in airtight jars for use as required. Here is a simple recipe for a *garam masala* to make at home.

Put all the ingredients in a heavy-bottomed frying pan and roast slowly until they are crisp and dry (or roast them in a low [275°F] oven), taking care that they do not burn. Grind them to a powder and store in an airtight jar in the refrigerator.

1 nutmeg, coarsely crushed

10-12 green cardamom pods

2-3 black cardamom pods

10-12 cloves

2 x 2-in pieces of cinnamon stick

2 tbsp cumin seeds

3-4 blades of mace

2-3 star anise

6-8 black peppercorns

4-5 bay leaves, crushed

Desserts and Drinks

Banana Fritters

Peel the bananas, cut them in half lengthwise and then cut each piece in half again across the middle. Melt the butter in a large frying pan over medium heat. Add the bananas flat-side down and sauté for 1½-2 minutes on each side, until pale golden. Don't let them become too soft. Remove the pan from the heat, place the bananas on individual serving plates and keep warm in a very low (250°F) oven.

Return the pan to medium-high heat. Add the sugar and stir to dissolve, then add the rum (resist temptation to overdo the rum or the sauce will get bitter or taste too sharp). Ignite the rum with a match or a lighter (standing far back) and allow it to burn for a few seconds. You may find that the sugar caramelizes into lumps. If that happens, remove the pan from the heat and cool slightly, then add a little cold water, stir to dissolve the sugar and return the pan to the heat.

Pour in the cream and shake the pan in a circular motion for a minute or so until the cream begins to boil. Stir gently with a wooden spatula until the sauce thickens a little. Spoon the sauce over the bananas and serve immediately.

4 large bananas

1 oz butter

3 tbsp demerara or dark brown granulated sugar

2-3 tbsp dark rum

5 fl oz light cream

Rawo is served on festive occasions as a good omen. Although it is traditionally prepared by women, please note that this is a man's version - mine. It makes a quick, simple and very tasty dessert and you will never again think of semolina as dull. You can decorate it with a few rose petals, if you like. Most rose petals are edible and they are widely used in India as a garnish on sweets, but make sure you choose unsprayed roses and soak them in water for a few minutes first.

Doodh No Rawo

PARSEE SEMOLINA PUDDING

1½ tbsp ghee
(or 1½ tsp butter and 2 tsp oil)

6 almonds, chopped

6 cashew nuts, chopped

1 tbsp golden raisins

½ oz butter

4 oz fine semolina

2½ tbsp sugar, or to taste

10 fl oz whole milk

¼ tsp grated nutmeg

¼ tsp ground cardamom

¼ tsp vanilla extract

½ tsp rose water

a pinch of saffron strands

Heat the *ghee* in a frying pan over medium heat, add the nuts and raisins and fry gently until the nuts are light golden. Transfer them into a sieve placed over a medium saucepan. Drain well, then place on paper towels to blot up any remaining fat.

Add the butter to the drained fat in the pan and melt over medium heat. As soon as the butter begins to foam, add the semolina. Reduce the heat slightly and roast the semolina, stirring constantly with a wooden spoon or spatula, for 7-8 minutes, until slightly colored. Be careful that it does not burn. Add the sugar and continue roasting for 4 minutes. Pour in the cold milk all at once and stir a bit faster now to prevent lumps. Simmer, stirring gently, for about 6-8 minutes, until the semolina is cooked. Add a little more milk if the mixture becomes too thick. It should have the consistency of thick porridge when removed from the heat, and will thicken further on cooling.

Stir in the nutmeg, cardamom, vanilla and rose water and cook for a minute or two, then taste and add more flavorings if necessary. You may also prefer to add more sugar; personally I don't like it very sweet.

Transfer to a serving bowl and sprinkle with the fried nuts and raisins. Serve warm. Leftover *rawo* is great even the following day and is good eaten cold as well.

TIP
Shake the chopped nuts in a sieve before frying. This way any small particles will be prevented from entering the fat and turning black.

Shahi Tukra

FRIED BREAD IN SAFFRON MILK

Heat the butter and oil in a large frying pan, add the bread, a few pieces at a time, and fry until golden brown on both sides. Transfer to a plate lined with paper towels to absorb excess fat.

Pour the milk into a heavy-bottomed saucepan and bring to a boil. Reduce the heat and simmer for 15-20 minutes, until it begins to change color. Stir regularly with a wooden spatula, scraping the bottom of the pan to prevent burning, and keep the sides of the pan clean with a pastry brush dipped in ice water as described on page 132. Add the sugar and continue cooking until the milk becomes light brown in color and gives off a nutty aroma. When the milk is ready it will be reduced in volume by at least a quarter and should coat the back of the spatula like a thin custard.

Stir in the saffron and cardamom and simmer for another 2 minutes. Now add the rose water and check the taste, adding more sugar if you feel it needs it. Let sit until warm.

Place the cold fried bread slices on a platter and pour over the warm milk. Decorate with the chopped nuts and let sit for 5-10 minutes, then serve. It is at its best when the bread is slightly crisp and not fully soaked.

1 oz butter

4 tbsp oil

4 slices of white bread, crusts removed, cut in half

17 fl oz whole milk

2 tbsp sugar, or to taste

a generous pinch of saffron strands

1/2 tsp ground cardamom

1 tsp rose water

2-3 almonds, chopped

12 pistachio nuts, chopped

Pronounced "alay baylay," this is a traditional Goan sweet and is thoroughly enjoyable served with vanilla ice cream, cream or custard.

Alle Belle

GOAN COCONUT PANCAKES

SERVES 6

4 oz all-purpose flour

1 tbsp superfine sugar

a pinch of salt

1 egg

5 fl oz coconut milk

1 tbsp melted butter, plus extra for brushing

a few drops of vanilla extract

a good pinch of grated lemon zest

a little oil or butter for frying

For the stuffing:

10-12 tbsp fresh or thawed frozen grated coconut (see page 96)

1 tbsp golden raisins

3 oz palm molasses or jaggery, coarsely grated

¼ tsp ground cardamom

¼ tsp grated nutmeg

Sift the flour, sugar and salt into a bowl, make a well in the center and add the egg, coconut milk and melted butter. Whisk to a smooth batter, then stir in the vanilla and lemon zest. It should have a thin pouring consistency.

Mix together all the ingredients for the stuffing.

Heat a little oil or butter in a 6-7-in frying pan. Pour in enough batter to coat the bottom thinly, tilting the pan to spread it. Cook for 1 minute, until lightly browned underneath, then flip over and cook the other side. Turn out and make the remaining pancakes in the same way.

Divide the filling between the pancakes and roll up. Place on individual serving plates, brush with melted butter and heat through under the broiler.

A sweet made by both Maharashtrians and Goans. It is very nutritious and is often given to nursing mothers. Recipes differ from region to region, so treat this one as a guide and use your imagination to come up with variations.

Sabu Daney Chey Aloney

SAGO WITH CARDAMOM AND COCONUT MILK

4 oz sago

8.5 fl oz whole milk

8 fl oz coconut milk (canned is fine)

5 oz granulated sugar, or to taste

a pinch of salt

5 green cardamom pods, crushed

1 tbsp ghee (or 1 tbsp oil and ½ tbsp butter)

2-3 tbsp golden raisins

10-15 cashew nuts, chopped

a few drops of vanilla extract and/or a few saffron strands (optional)

Optional decoration:

chopped pistachios and almonds

freshly grated nutmeg

Wash the sago lightly, put it in a bowl and add enough water to cover by about ¾ in. Let soak for 15 minutes. Drain through a colander, place in a heavy-bottomed saucepan and add the milk, coconut milk, sugar, salt and crushed cardamom. Bring gently to a boil and simmer, stirring frequently to prevent sticking, for 15-20 minutes or until all the milk has been absorbed and the sago is swollen and translucent.

Meanwhile, heat the *ghee* in a pan, add the raisins and cashew nuts and fry until the nuts are golden brown. If there is any fat left in the pan, drain the nuts and raisins through a small sieve. If all the fat has been absorbed, place them on paper towels to blot them dry.

Taste the sago and add more sugar if necessary. You could also add some vanilla extract and, better still, a few threads of saffron. Stir in the raisins and cashew nuts.

Pour the mixture into individual lightly buttered ramekins and leave for about 5 minutes, then turn out onto a platter while still warm. Decorate with chopped pistachios and almonds and/or grated nutmeg, if you like. Serve warm or cold.

This may sound a bit weird but in fact it tastes really good. However, if you are very calorie conscious it is best to steer clear, or feed it to your friends instead.

Eeda Paak

EGG FUDGE

Lightly beat the eggs, then put them in a heavy-bottomed non-stick pan with the sugar, butter, 4 tablespoons of ground almonds, rose water, vanilla, cardamom, nutmeg and cream. Stir over low heat with a wooden spatula, then when everything is well blended increase the heat slightly. Stir constantly, right up from the bottom of the pan or the egg will tend to settle and form lumps. After about 20 minutes the mixture should be very thick and pulling away from the sides of the pan (if it is still not thick enough, stir in the extra tablespoon of ground almonds).

Transfer to a greased 7-in square baking pan and level the top. Sprinkle with the nuts and press them down a bit. Leave until warm, then mark into $3/4$-in squares with a spatula. When completely cool, cut right through the squares and remove from the pan. The fudge will keep covered in the refrigerator for a few weeks. For the best flavor, warm it slightly before serving.

6 large eggs

7 oz superfine sugar

$4^1/_2$ oz butter

4–5 heaping tbsp ground almonds

2 tbsp rose water

a few drops of vanilla extract

6 cardamom pods, ground, or $^1/_4$ tsp ready-ground cardamom

$^3/_4$ tsp grated nutmeg

2 tbsp heavy cream

1–2 tbsp chopped mixed nuts

Parsee Pav Makhan Nu Pudding

RICH PARSEE-STYLE BREAD AND BUTTER PUDDING

SERVES 4-6

35 fl oz whole milk

5 eggs

5-7 oz granulated sugar, plus extra for sprinkling

1 tbsp rose water

½ tsp vanilla extract

½ tsp ground cardamom

½ tsp grated nutmeg

plenty of butter

5-6 slices of white bread

1 tbsp golden raisins

1½ tbsp chopped mixed dried fruit

12-15 almonds, chopped

1 tbsp charoli (if not available, substitute pistachios)

Bring the milk to a boil in a heavy-bottomed saucepan, then simmer gently for about half an hour, keeping the sides of the pan clean at all times. To do this, immediately after the milk has reduced to a simmer, dip a pastry brush into a bowl of ice water and brush down the sides of the pan. Repeat this every few minutes but make sure the brush is not dripping wet or it will dilute the milk. This might seem very time-consuming but it does give the milk a better flavor. Scrape the bottom of the pan frequently with a wooden spatula. The milk should eventually turn a shade darker and give off a nutty/toffeeish aroma. When it is ready it will be reduced by at least a quarter and should coat the back of the spatula like a thin custard. Remove from the heat and leave until warm.

Beat the eggs and sugar together until light and foamy - start off with a small amount of sugar, then taste after the milk has been added to see if you prefer it sweeter. Gradually whisk in the warm milk, then whisk for a minute. Mix in the rose water, vanilla extract, cardamom and nutmeg.

Generously butter a baking dish about 50 fl oz in capacity and then sprinkle it with sugar until well coated. Butter the bread slices on both sides (trimming the crusts off if you prefer) and arrange half of them in a single layer in the dish, trimming them to fit. Sprinkle the raisins and mixed fruit on top, then cover with the remaining bread and pour in the egg mixture. Sprinkle with the almonds and *charoli* and place in an oven preheated to 400°F. Bake for 10 minutes, then reduce the temperature to 350°F and bake for 15-20 minutes or until a knife inserted in the center comes out clean. The pudding should be golden and crisp on top; if necessary broil it under low heat to brown. Serve warm or cold.

As a kid I used to love this poured over hot *chapatis*, and the habit never died. If you like golden or maple syrup, this is a delicious new twist. Pour it over toast and enjoy it for breakfast, or serve with ice cream.

Gor No Seero

JAGGERY SYRUP

16 oz jaggery
7 fl oz water

Cut up the jaggery into small pieces or shavings. Place it in a bowl and pour the water over. Microwave on high for 5 minutes or until the jaggery is totally dissolved and the mixture is boiling. Cool slightly, then strain through a cheesecloth-lined sieve. Bottle the syrup and store.

You can also make the syrup in a pan on the stove: heat slowly until the jaggery has dissolved into the water, then boil for 5-6 minutes and strain.

Some types of jaggery absorb less water than others and the syrup may become too thin. If this happens, simply add more jaggery and simmer in a pan set over low heat until dissolved.

Like good honey, jaggery tends to crystallize in the jar. Just warm it up before use, either in the microwave or by standing the jar in hot water.

Lassi

Lassi is a beaten yogurt drink. It is quite substantial and many Indians would drink a good *lassi* in summer and not eat afterwards, or simply have a light snack. It is essential to use good-quality, creamy yogurt, such as Greek-style. In India buffalo milk yogurt, which has a 12-14 percent fat content, is normally used; remember that low-fat yogurt will not achieve the same lipsmacking result.

MANGO LASSI

To make this popular *lassi*, take about 5 fl oz yogurt, $\frac{1}{4}$ glass of canned mango pulp (or 1 fresh mango, peeled, pitted and chopped), 4 ice cubes and some sugar if necessary. Place everything in a blender and give it a good whirl. Pour out into a tall glass and enjoy.

Other fruit such as strawberries, raspberries or papaya can be used.

MASALA LASSI

Put 5-7 oz plain yogurt in a blender with a $\frac{1}{2}$-in piece of fresh ginger root, $\frac{1}{4}$ teaspoon of cumin seeds (preferably roasted - see page 14), a small piece of mild green chili, 2-3 curry leaves, a pinch each of salt and sugar and a few ice cubes. Process until smooth, then serve with a sprinkling of very finely chopped fresh mint and cilantro. You could try puréeing the herbs with the *lassi* but you may find the flavor an acquired taste.

JEERA LASSI

Blend 5-7 oz yogurt with $\frac{1}{2}$ teaspoon of cumin seeds (preferably roasted - see page 14), some salt and a few ice cubes. Both this and the Masala Lassi are good for upset stomachs, acidity and general digestive discomfort.

SWEET LASSI

Just yogurt and ice cubes blended with a little sugar.

Limbu Panis

FRESH LIME WATER

This is sold in almost every major street of every large city in India. Fresh lime water is as popular as *lassi* but lighter and more refreshing. It helps to replace lost fluids and to control dehydration and nausea brought about by the extreme heat.

To make a simple *limbu panis*, put 2 tablespoons of freshly squeezed lime juice in a glass with 2-3 teaspoons of sugar and a pinch of salt. Add a little water and mix well until the sugar dissolves, then top up with ice water. Use soda water for a fizzy drink, if you prefer.

Salt and ground cumin are sometimes added. In India *kala namak*, or black rock salt, is used in the summer months to help prevent dehydration.

Tarbooj Ka Pani

FRESH WATERMELON JUICE

Peel and seed a large piece of watermelon, being sure to remove all the seeds. Process the flesh in a blender with a few ice cubes, then transfer to a bowl. Stir in raspberry cordial to taste. Rock salt may be added too, if you like.

By the Stock Exchange in Bombay, frantic brokers guzzle down cup upon cup of spiced tea every day. Different flavors and sizes are prepared according to demand.

A simple recipe is given here that will not only perk you up on a cold, dreary morning but also clear that unwanted crackle in sore throats. It doesn't matter what sort of tea you use but a small-leaf variety is best; don't go for anything particularly exclusive. The milk should be whole milk; skimmed does not give the same result. In India we use rich, creamy buffalo milk.

Masala Cha

SPICED TEA

Put a mixture of half milk/half water in a saucepan (quantities will depend on how many cups you are making). For every 2-3 cups, add 4-6 cardamom pods and a $\frac{1}{2}$-in piece of fresh ginger, flattened with a heavy knife handle. Bring to a boil, simmer for a minute and then add the tea leaves - a little less than you would if you were making tea in a pot. Simmer for 3-5 minutes. Remove from the heat, cover and leave to infuse for a few minutes, then strain into the cups.

VARIATIONS
- A pinch of ground ginger or crushed peppercorns can be added when the tea is left to infuse.

- One clove for every 3 cups is sometimes included.

- A few saffron strands, some ground pistachios and ground cardamom can be stirred in after the tea is strained.

- A bruised fresh lemongrass stalk and a couple of mint leaves can be added when the tea is left to infuse. A 3-in single layer of lemongrass is sufficient to flavor 3 cups.

- A small stick of cinnamon will yield yet another unique flavor, much enjoyed by the Pakistani people.

Glossary

Amchur
This is powdered mango, made by peeling, sun-drying and grinding unripe mangoes. It is one of the ingredients of *chaat masala* and is also used to flavor salads and chickpea and bean dishes.

Asafetida (*Hing*)
The sun-dried gum of the ferula (a type of giant fennel), this used to come in a hard lump but is now more widely sold as a powder. Asafetida is an anti-flatulent so it is often added to bean dishes. It is also used for other purposes in Ayurvedic medicine.

Besan
Besan is a chickpea flour used to make *pakoras* and *bhajias* and as a thickening agent for dishes such as *kadhi* (see page 88). It is also used in various sweets and fudges.

Cardamom (*Elaichi*)
Known as the queen of spices, cardamom is extensively used throughout India in meat, poultry, game and vegetarian dishes as well as sweets and desserts. The best cardamom comes from Kerala in southwest India. There are many varieties but the most popular is the green. The brown cardamom, which is also used in Indian cooking, has large pods with a fibrous skin somewhat like a mini coconut.

Carom seeds (*Ajwain*)
These small brown seeds look like tiny cumin. They are used to make poultices to numb the pain from toothache; in fact some medicinal mouthwashes taste strongly of carom. Because of their powerful flavor it is best to use them sparingly in cooking. They are added to batters and used to flavor green vegetables and *pulaos*.

Channa daal
Channa daal is a type of split chickpea but is sometimes confused with yellow split peas, which come from the same family and have a very similar flavor. Very popular in Punjab and the northern states, it is also used in southern and central Indian cooking, particularly in Kerala, where it is made into a sweet for one of its best-known festivals, the *Onam*.

Charoli
Also known as *chironji* in Hindi, this is the tiny kernel of the fruit of the same name. It most resembles a small bean and has a peculiar flavor – sweetish and almost musky. Used primarily as a garnish, it is not readily available outside India, although some Indian markets may stock it. It is not widely used in India but since the Gujeratis love it you are likely to find it in stores run by them.

Chili
Hari mirch, laal mirch, mirsang and *marcha* are some of the names by which this venerable member of the capsicum family is known in India. It is perhaps the most widely used ingredient in Indian cooking today, and very few savory dishes require no chili at all.

The Portuguese are credited with introducing chilies to India, although I find this hard to believe. They may well have brought with them from South America some of the varieties that grow in Goa today but surely they couldn't have been responsible for the countless different types of chili cultivated in India.

In the past, chilies were reputed to have medicinal properties and they are indeed rich sources of vitamins A and C. Their heat comes from a volatile oil called capsaicin. Generally, the smaller chilies are more lethal than their larger, plumper cousins (although this cannot always be relied upon). For this reason I tend to specify large chilies in my recipes.

I like to use fresh green chilies to add a last-minute zing to savory dishes and chutneys, while dried red chilies are more useful as a spice. In Indian cooking they are cut up and fried to release their flavor before other spices are added, and may be ground to make a *masala*.

Cilantro (see Coriander)

Coconut (*Narial*)
Selecting a good coconut is crucial to Indians. The choice is more limited outside India, but look for a heavy nut that makes a good deep sound when tapped with a ring on your finger or your keys. Try out the sound of different coconuts to help you decide. Then shake it close to your ear and listen for the telltale sloshing of liquid inside. If the coconut doesn't contain much liquid it will not be very good for cooking. The giant coconuts from the west coast of Goa are the best I have ever eaten but unfortunately they are seldom available elsewhere.

Coconut oil (*Narial ka tel*)
Extracted from dried coconut, this is available in various forms. Select a refined version if you are not familiar with the taste of coconut in your food. Coconut oil is very strong and should always be used with discretion. It is popular in southern India and Goa for cooking but is, in fact, primarily used as a hair oil. It makes an excellent massage oil and is also used in religious ceremonies.

Cokum
Sometimes referred to in English as the butternut berry, this is the small, round, deep purple fruit of a large evergreen tree and has a tart flavor. It is very versatile and is used extensively in Gujerat, Maharashtra and Goa – less so in other parts of India. It is regarded as a very good

tonic for stomach disorders and skin ailments. Primarily used these days for flavoring curries, it is also sold as a syrup for making a delightful summer drink. Most Indian markets should stock dried *cokums*, but if you cannot find them, use a tart variety of plum instead.

Colcasia leaves (*Arbi, arvi na patra*)
Arbi is a root vegetable that is widely used throughout India but especially in the north. The large, heart-shaped leaves are also used in cooking – one of the best known dishes is *patra*, or *patrel* as Parsees call it, where the leaves are stuffed with lentils and steamed, then sliced and eaten fried or cold. One or two leaves can be added to *dhansak* for flavor, although they are not essential.

Coriander (*Dhania*)
Both coriander seeds and the fresh green leaves (cilantro) are essential ingredients in Indian cooking. The seeds are valued not only for their flavor but also for their medicinal properties. The quality of ready-ground coriander is very good nowadays, but for the best flavor you still need to grind the seeds yourself. Always roast them gently first (see page 14), then grind them to the consistency you prefer. Crushed roasted cumin and coriander can be used together as a condiment, added to dishes in the final stages of cooking to give them a lift.

Fresh coriander, or cilantro, is an extremely versatile herb, not only in Indian cooking but in Western dishes too. Try substituting it for spinach in eggs Florentine for a delicious and unusual variation.

Cumin (*Jeera*)
This warm, sweetish yet slightly bitter spice has found its way into every corner of Indian cooking and it also has useful medicinal properties. The seeds are generally roasted to bring out their flavor (see page 14). To store cumin, keep it in an airtight jar, preferably

in the refrigerator, where it will keep fresh for months.

Curry leaves (*Kadi patta*)
These small, oval leaves come from the *Murraya koenigii* plant, which eventually grows into a tree. They have a lovely powerful aroma and can be used fresh or dried, although dried ones do not have the same intense flavor.

If you can only find dried ones, you will need to use more of them. When you come across fresh curry leaves it is worth freezing them whole and using them direct from the freezer.

Drumstick (*Sekta ni singh, muska chey sango*)
This long, slender bean from an evergreen tree has a unique flavor, quite unlike anything else. Its stringy texture and very hard skin make it impossible to eat whole, so it is usually cut into sections and added to curries for flavor, then peeled before eating. You should be able to find it in Indian markets.

Fenugreek (*Methi*)
Classed as a spinach in India, fenugreek is rich in iron, minerals and vitamins. It has small, oval, bitter-tasting leaves and is sold in India as a two-stage crop: the very tender young leaves resemble mustard cress in appearance and have a powerful flavor; the larger leaves are less strong and are cooked as a vegetable with meat and other greens.

Dried fenugreek is used extensively and could be said to act as the monosodium glutamate of northern Indian cooking. It is usually toasted first to mellow the flavor (see page 9).

Fenugreek seeds are used as a spice and are also very bitter, with a strong curry flavor. They are fried or roasted before use to reduce the pungency.

Garlic (*Lehsun, lasab, losun*)
Commonly believed in Indian folklore to be a destroyer of evil spirits, garlic is highly valued for its medicinal and culinary properties. It is an indispensable addition to most

Indian dishes. In some parts of India, fresh green garlic is very popular and can be used to make excellent scrambled eggs.

Store garlic in a dry, airy place but do not leave it in the dark for too long or it will sprout, giving it a bitter flavor.

Ghee
Ghee is a form of clarified butter, traditionally prepared from homemade butter. In India, since buffalo milk is more commonly used than cow's milk and is very rich, a great deal of cream is collected in the house. Sometimes this is cooked slowly until only the fat remains, to make another form of *ghee*.

Ghee is available in two forms – pure *ghee*, made from butter, and vegetable *ghee*. Very pure *ghee* seldom solidifies.

Ginger (*Adrak, aadoo*)
This versatile root is added to just about everything from curries, spice blends, dressings and pickles to jams, sweets and drinks.

Ginger is an excellent tenderizer and is widely used as such in Indian cooking, particularly in tandoori marinades. Parsee households cannot do without ginger, sometimes even adding it to their tea (see page 137).

Green banana (*Kachcha kela*)
Green bananas and green plantains (which are larger and starchier than bananas) are used widely in Indian cooking, particularly by the Gujeratis, Maharashtrians, Goans and in southern India. However, the cooking methods vary greatly.

Green bananas and plantains are sold in many supermarkets, as well as Indian markets in the U.S., and you will also find a good choice in West Indian markets. They are often cooked in their skins to keep the flesh intact.

Jaggery (*Good*)
Jaggery (also known as palm sugar) is an unrefined sugar made in rural areas of India by boiling down sugar cane juice in large

kadhai-type pans. It is used widely to make desserts and sweets and is also added to many savory dishes. It is sold in blocks and has a delicious fudge-like flavor. You should be able to find it in most Indian markets. If you cannot get it, Demerara sugar is the best substitute, although the flavor cannot be compared.

Jaggery made from palm toddy is also available in the south of India, including Goa, and is much darker with a distinctly different flavor.

Kabuli channa

These are simply large white chickpeas - the kind that are also popular in the Middle East and are readily available elsewhere, either canned or dried. They are cultivated in the north of India, with the best-known chickpea dishes coming from the Punjab. In many parts of India they are known as *bengal gram*.

Khus-khus

Khus-khus, or white poppy seeds, are added to curries and kormas, both as a thickening agent and for their flavor. It is important to avoid stale seeds as they may taste rancid.

As a young child I spent some time in Madhya Pradesh/Rajasthan, where poppies were cultivated as a source of opium. The dried seeds were widely used in cooking and in those days we had to buy the entire bulb. The seeds rattled inside, making a *khus-khus* sound, which perhaps explains the name. I lived in a town called Neemuch, where a strong smell wafted in regularly from the world's largest opium refinery nearby. This ensured that you slept extremely well and never suffered from a stuffy nose.

Masoor daal

These small red or pink lentils are very versatile and easy to cook. They are used extensively in Indian cooking, from starters through to desserts.

Moong daal

These are mung beans. They can be cooked like any other beans but always remain slightly firm, so are seldom puréed. They are often used on religious occasions. A *moong kheer*, for example, may be served at a ceremony or at the beginning of a celebratory meal. They can be made into a delicious tasty snack known as *mogar* by first soaking them and then roasting them in a wok or *kadhai* with a very little oil.

Mustard oil *(Sarsoon ka tel)*

This strongly flavored oil has a pungent smell and is very viscous. It is popular in northern Indian cooking, particularly Bengal and the Punjab, whereas the south is dominated by coconut oil. Mustard oil is primarily used for making pickles. If you are using it in cooking it is best to heat it to smoking point, add a couple of red chilies and then remove from the heat. When cool, discard the chilies and use the oil as desired. This process mellows the pungent aroma and flavor.

Mustard oil is also used as a liniment and in several massage oils. As a hair tonic, it is thought to promote good, strong, lustrous, healthy hair.

Mustard seeds *(Rai dana, sarsoon, sansua)*

Though several varieties of mustard seeds are grown in India, the black ones are the most common. They have an excellent flavor when tempered. Mustard also has several medicinal applications and is widely used in the preparation of dishes for religious festivals.

Palm vinegar *(Taadi no sarco, boorachey vinaigir)*

Also known as toddy vinegar, this is the juice of the palm tree. The tree has a sort of a jugular vein which is tapped so that a milky fluid is released into pots tied beneath. The liquid is collected overnight and then drunk early in the morning. After midday it begins to ferment vigorously and becomes undrinkable. It is then used for making bread and the remainder is stored in vats and matured into vinegar. A spirit is also distilled from the must and is known as *feni* in Goa and *arrak* in southern India. Toddy is warmed and served to invalids, particularly pneumonia patients. The taste is disgusting and it is little wonder that even though the British adopted the term 'hot toddy' they decided to give the patient whisky and hot water instead. Toddy vinegar is available in Filipino and other Asian markets. It is not really suitable for Western-style cooking but is an essential ingredient in *piri-piri*, *balchao* and *patia*.

Paneer

Paneer is a simple fresh whey cheese. Its texture varies according to how it is made. For instance, Parsees make their *paneer* soft and creamy or set it in tiny cane baskets immersed in brine, like fresh mozzarella only softer and more delicate. The Punjabi-style *paneer* is the best known outside India. The whey cheese is pressed down with a heavy pot so that it becomes firm and hard. See page 81 for information on preparing this sort of *paneer* for cooking.

Rice

Chawal, chokha, dhan, xit (pronounced *zeet*), *tandul* - these are just some of the names by which rice is known in India. The Western world has come to think that there is only one rice in India - basmati. In fact there are hundreds of varieties and basmati is the least consumed. Such large quantities are exported that it has become too expensive for the average Indian to afford. It has always been a rice for special occasions because of its delicate flavor and aroma. However, several other varieties are equally treasured, some of which I find even more special - for example, *kolum*, or the silky one from Gujerat, and *amba mohur*, meaning mango blossom. It is fortunate that most of these are virtually unknown outside India and so have preserved their unique qualities, free from hybrid strains or intensive cultivation.

Another myth about rice is that it

is a staple food throughout India. It certainly is in the south, in regions such as Goa, Tamil Nadu, Kerala and Karnataka, and in most parts of Maharashtra, but in the northwest, where basmati is cultivated, wheat is the staple grain.

Most rice in India is aged before it is sold, and the older the rice the greater the value – just as with good wine. To judge rice, take a little in the palm of one hand and rub it with your other thumb to warm it. Then sniff it, as you would a good wine or spirit, rub again and sniff again. A good rice will give off a distinct aroma, which will give a connoisseur an indication of its age. An expert will also be able to tell this from the texture of the grain. With any rice it is worth checking that there are not too many broken grains and that it is not riddled with specks of white.

If you manage to buy really good rice from an Indian market (it will be packed in a gunny bag, a sack made from jute), remember that it will need washing and soaking thoroughly before cooking – unlike the well-known prepackaged brands, which are heavily polished. Once opened, keep the remaining rice sealed in an airtight container.

If you are a rice enthusiast, then do try the wonderful range that is now available. We use red rice from the Camargue region of France and several organic Italian varieties daily in the restaurant and also like to try the Asian ones. All in all, rice is the grain of God to millions and should be revered accordingly.

Sev

Sev is chickpea vermicelli, available from most Indian markets. A stiff dough is made from chickpea flour, then squeezed through a press into hot oil and fried until crisp. The sev is broken up and sold either on its own or mixed with other ingredients to make chewda, or sev ganthia – known as Bombay mix for some reason.

Shrimp powder (Sukay suncta cho pito)

Used as a flavoring in Goan dishes and Asian curries, shrimp powder is also very popular in Burmese cooking. It is available in jars from Asian markets, sometimes mixed with crushed dried chili. If you buy dried shrimp or prawns, you can make your own shrimp powder by roasting them very slowly. When cold they turn crisp and can then be powdered in a small grinder.

Snakegourd (Padwal)

This is a long, thin, gently curved green vegetable like a slender crooked marrow. In the north of India it is particularly enjoyed with pulses, while in the south it is used in mixed vegetable dishes such as sambhar. Snakegourd should be peeled, then split open, seeded and cut into chunks before cooking. It cooks very rapidly.

Star anise (Badian, fool patri)

It is thought that the Chinese introduced this aniseed-flavored spice to India. It is not very widely used in Indian cooking but many chefs add it to their garam masala and Parsees use it to flavor brown rice and occasionally in chutneys.

Tamarind (Imli)

This brown, bean-shaped pod of a tropical plant is a very important ingredient throughout India, imparting a unique tart flavor to food. Chutneys, curries, sauces, pulses, vegetables and rice dishes all benefit from the gentle touch of tamarind, added at the beginning of cooking or at the very end. It is also popular as a snack during school breaks. Tamarind vendors can often be seen outside schools selling fresh tamarind with a bag of salt and chili powder as a dip. It is very sour eaten like this but children love it. Tamarind is also highly valued for its unique medicinal properties and is a particularly rich source of vitamin C. You will find it in Indian markets and some large supermarkets, sold as a compressed block, a concentrate or a paste. See page 28 for information on preparing tamarind.

Toover daal

These large yellow lentils are very common throughout India and are the most popular daal of all. There are a few varieties available and you may also see them with castor oil added to prevent them from going rancid or succumbing to weevils.

Always store your lentils in an airtight jar and wash them thoroughly before cooking until the water turns clear. Toover daal is good on its own or mixed with other pulses.

Turmeric (Haldi/Harad)

This aromatic member of the ginger family is most readily available dried, either in its root form or ground to a powder, but it can also be bought fresh in some Asian markets. The fresh root is a deep orange shade, only achieving its characteristic yellow color when dried. Turmeric is a well-known antiseptic and has several uses in Indian medicine (see page 42).

Urad daal

These are black gram beans, eaten either whole (very popular in northern India, especially the Punjab) or hulled and split to give a white bean (more popular in Madhya Pradesh and Rajasthan). When cooked, the split beans are unusually sticky and starchy. Do not overcook them or try to purée them or they will become glutinous, resembling a gruel rather than a daal.

Watana

These are dried white peas (actually a pale yellow color) and are used throughout central and northern India. They need to be well soaked before cooking. If you are in a hurry, add a teaspoon of baking powder or bicarbonate of soda to the cooking water.

Index